Better Homes and Gardens®

Grandma's Best
FULL-SIZE
Quilt Blocks

Pieces of the Past for Today's Quilter

Better Homes and Gardens® Books ⬥ Des Moines, Iowa

Pieces of the Past

I made quilts as fast as I could to keep my family warm, and as pretty as I could to keep my heart from breaking.
—A PIONEER WOMAN'S DIARY

The first real quilt I remember making happened quite by chance. My Grandmother was sorting through her closet one day when I stopped there after school. She reached up to the top dusty shelf of the closet and found a shoebox filled with appliquéd butterfly blocks. "Oh, these were Mother's," she said. "I think I remember how this quilt was supposed to go together." We laid out the blocks on her hardwood floor, carefully deciding what colors would be most pleasing between them. I remember asking Grandma about the tiny prints that were used to create the happy butterflies and discovering that they were indeed pieces of the past, dresses that she and her sister had worn. She told me about the colorful prints, reliving the events that she remembered about each special design.

That butterfly-appliquéd quilt trimmed with fresh yellow sashings covered the bed in my daughter's room for years. She would touch her favorite prints and giggle at the butterflies when she was a toddler. Her hands would reach for the butterflies near her when she was sick, and she snuggled under the warmth of that quilt when the winters were cold. As she grew, she would lie across the bed, outlining the butterflies with her fingers as she did her homework or talked on the phone with her friends.

Grandma is gone now, and my daughter is nearly grown up. The quilt is a bit tattered and I'm told that I probably shouldn't have actually used it on her bed for all those growing up years or let her sit on it and touch each aging print. But somehow I think Great-Grandma would have loved to have her giggle, snuggle, and touch each cheerful butterfly as she fell fast asleep.

Quilting is more than measuring and sewing and being precise and careful. It is about making warmth and beauty for the people you love most. For generations, women have continued to care for their families through good times and bad. In this book we've offered you a glimpse of exquisite quilts from years past, many from never-before-seen collections. And we've adapted and created designs to give you full-size blocks and borders that you can make from your favorite fabrics. We've shown you two ways that we made the blocks—one using vintage or reproduction fabrics, and one with fabrics we just happen to love—and we give you ideas for how to put the blocks together. We even give you complete instructions, including yardages, patterns, and tips, for making some of the antique quilts just as you see them in this book. Finally, we hope that by showing some of Grandma's best quilts we inspire you to join the ranks of the talented and caring women before us who used their extraordinary skills to create lasting warmth and beauty for generations to come.

Carol Field Dahlstrom

Contents

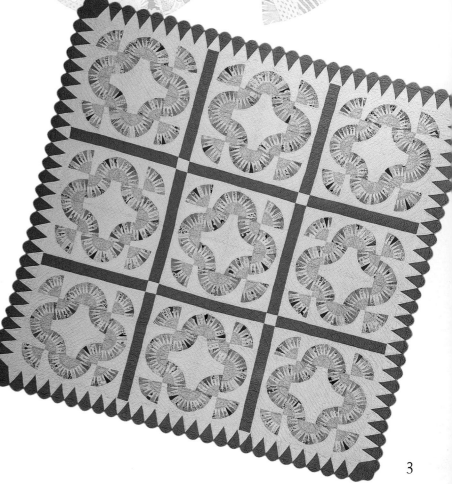

Features in the Book

The Inspiration for the Quilts

The 101 quilt blocks and borders in this book are inspired by breathtaking vintage quilts dating from 1830 to 1950. To find such inspiration we searched the country for quilts that accurately and exquisitely exemplified the time period in which they were created. We visited museums and universities and located individual collectors who so graciously shared their enthusiasm and expertise with us. We give a special thanks to the International Quilt Study Center at the University of Nebraska–Lincoln, and curator Carolyn Ducey who shared their exquisite collection with us. Many of the quilts you

EXQUISITE ANTIQUE QUILTS ARE USED AS INSPIRATION FOR THE DOZENS OF FULL-SIZE QUILT BLOCKS SHOWN.

see in this book are from that collection and have inspired many of the blocks in the book. This collection was given to the University as a gift from Ardis and Robert James, formerly of Nebraska. More about this collection from the Jameses and a numerical list of each quilt shown in the book can be found on *pages 214–215*.

We also would like to thank Deb Irving and Living History Farms in Des Moines, Iowa who so kindly shared their collection and expertise on vintage quilts and fabrics with us. Many of the period photos were photographed at the Farms. For more information about the Living History Farms, *see page 214.*

These collections, along with quilts from individual collectors, served as the inspiration for the blocks and borders you'll find in this book. We have also given you complete instructions for many of the antique quilts you see in this book. Each of the featured quilts tells a story—about a period in history, about the quilters' labors, and about the fabrics, styles, colors, and popular motifs of the time.

The Quilts

From elaborate appliqué to intricate pieced works, the selection of quilts in this book will inspire quilters to new heights. The quilts are arranged by time periods: 1830 to 1860, 1860 to 1890, 1890 to 1920, and 1920 to 1950. Some of the vintage quilts were mere inspiration for the quilt blocks that follow in that chapter. Some have been chosen to reflect the historic time in which they are given. All of the blocks have been adapted to 9-inch size.

9-INCH BLOCK PATTERNS (ABOVE) AND 2 DIFFERENT BLOCK COLOR OPTIONS FOR EACH BLOCK DESIGN (BELOW)

The Blocks

This book includes 70 blocks to be re-created and used in a multitude of quilting projects. Each of the blocks is 9 inches and has two color options. The first sample uses fabrics similar to the original in inspiration or appropriate for that time period. The second option shows another color palette that changes the look of the block. All the blocks were inspired by a vintage quilt or were designed to complement the time period when they appear.

Full-size patterns are provided for each block as well as complete instructions and an assembly option. **When using the pattern pieces, a ¼-inch seam allowance needs to be added to all pieces** *unless they are to be machine appliquéd.* For hand-appliquéd

QUILT ASSEMBLY IDEAS FOR EACH BLOCK

blocks, appliqué pieces can be cut with a
$\frac{3}{16}$-inch seam allowance so the turned-back
portion is not too bulky. If a piece is
reversed, it is labeled with an "r" after the
corresponding pattern piece letter.

COMBINING THE BLOCKS

For each quilt block there is an assembly
diagram to show an interesting option for
combining the blocks. This assembly
diagram may be different than the quilt that
inspired the block. There are ideas for
sashings, setting the blocks on point,
borders, and combinations using more than
one block design.

Throughout these assembly diagrams
there are various size quilts—from crib to
king size. If a different size is desired, you
can redesign the quilt by adding or deleting
blocks, sashings, or borders. It is this
flexibility that adds your personal creativity
to the finished work. The instructions
("How to Make This Quilt") are provided
by each assembly diagram.

Because all of the blocks are 9 inches,
they can be interchanged with one
another to create the look you like.

THE BORDERS

The last chapter in the book offers several
pieced and appliquéd quilt borders to finish
your quilt. You'll notice that they are used
throughout the book on the assembly option
diagrams. These borders are again inspired
by vintage quilts photographed in the book.

THE FABRICS

In each time period there is information
about the fabrics that quilters used during
that time in history. Along with interesting
photographs of actual vintage fabrics, you'll
discover which fabrics, colors, and prints
were popular and readily available during a
specified time period.

For historical interest, photographs of
other household items—sewing notions,
glassware, books, and more—from the
various time periods are shown. These
items would have been used and enjoyed
by quilters and their families.

THE EMBELLISHMENTS

Embroidery stitches were often used to add
intricate detail to quilts, especially crazy quilts.
On *page 199* you'll find diagrams for a handful
of stitches that have been traditionally
stitched on quilts for ornamentation.

PATTERNS AND
INSTRUCTIONS
ARE GIVEN TO
RE-CREATE BORDERS
TO FINISH YOUR QUILTS.

VINTAGE QUILTS ARE FEATURED IN EACH ERA.
FULL-SIZE PATTERNS, YARDAGES, AND FULL
INSTRUCTIONS ARE PROVIDED FOR MANY OF
THE ANTIQUE QUILTS SHOWN.

FABRIC SAMPLES FROM EACH HISTORIC PERIOD ARE SHOWN.

1830-1860

W ith the hardships that the colonists faced as they moved westward came a dawning of great promise and opportunity. As families claimed their prairie land, women took to their quilting. Wholecloth quilts began to be replaced with pieced quilts and elegant album quilts. New American and imported fabrics became available, and the patchwork block became a practical way for quilters to combine order and beauty.

Period Quilt History

Early settlers in America brought with them the skills and styles of their European homelands. They were familiar with wholecloth coverlets and garments quilted with hearts, feathers, and other traditional motifs. In addition to making wholecloth counterpanes, affluent women made quilts by appliquéing chintz cutouts onto plain backgrounds in the *broderie perse* (Persian embroidery) style.

In the early 1800s, pieced and appliquéd quilts were made with central medallions surrounded by a series of borders. The first patchwork designs were simple geometric patterns based on basic shapes—squares and right triangles.

During the mid-1800s, new fabrics and economic conditions raised patchwork to unparalleled heights in America. Early in the 19th century, America had its own textile industry. (The first cotton textile plant opened in 1790 at Pawtucket, Rhode Island.) The flood of inexpensive and washable cottons unleashed creativity in quiltmaking. Although American quiltmakers continued to make broderie perse and medallion quilts, they began to develop a new concept—the use of small individual blocks.

The proliferation of patchwork block design, among the most significant developments in quiltmaking, is a purely American phenomenon. Blocks made one at a time and joined together were practical, yet met the maker's need for order and beauty. Through quilting bees, prolific

ALBUM QUILT
c.1850

THE TAG THAT ACCOMPANIES THIS QUILT READS: "ORIGINALLY BELONGED TO WILLIAM BUCHAN, BROTHER OF BERNICE OLSON'S GRANDMOTHER JORDAN. MADE BY GIRLFRIENDS AND NEIGHBORS, EACH PIECING ONE BLOCK; AUBURN, ILLINOIS." A LIVELY SERPENTINE BORDER SURROUNDS THE APPLIQUÉ AND TRAPUNTO WORK. FULL INSTRUCTIONS ARE NOT AVAILABLE FOR THIS QUILT. FOR THE BLOCK INSPIRED BY THIS QUILT, SEE PAGE 47. *Courtesy: University of Nebraska-Lincoln*

NINE-PATCH QUILT
c.1845

ATTACHED TO THIS NINE-PATCH QUILT IS A TAG THAT READS: "MADE BY GREAT-GRANDMA AND GIVEN TO FATHER YEARS AGO—I DON'T KNOW, EVER SINCE I CAN REMEMBER." THE RAINBOW-QUILTED VERMONT QUILT USES A NINE-PATCH CENTER IN EACH BLOCK FRAMED BY RECTANGLES AND BRIGHT GREEN CORNERS. RED AND BROWN FABRICS DOMINATE WITH ACCENTS OF BLUE. EACH BLOCK IS BORDERED BY MULTICOLOR FLYING GEESE. FULL INSTRUCTIONS ARE NOT AVAILABLE FOR THIS QUILT. FOR THE BLOCK INSPIRED BY THE QUILT, SEE PAGE 22. *Courtesy: University of Nebraska-Lincoln*

FRIENDSHIP ALBUM QUILT
c. 1851

THIS FRIENDSHIP ALBUM QUILT IS SIGNED PHILADELPHIA, PENNSYLVANIA, ELIZABETHTOWN, NEW JERSEY, AND NEW YORK. THE AMERICAN, FRENCH, AND SWEDISH FLAGS ARE FEATURED AMONG AN INTERESTING MIX OF FLORAL, GEOMETRIC, AND ABSTRACT SHAPES. THE DATES AND LOCATIONS INSCRIBED IN INDIA INK ON VARIOUS QUILT BLOCKS INDICATE THAT IT TOOK THREE YEARS TO COLLECT THEM, A USUAL LENGTH OF TIME TO PRODUCE THE ELABORATE WORK. FULL INSTRUCTIONS ARE NOT AVAILABLE FOR THIS QUILT. FOR BLOCKS INSPIRED BY THIS QUILT, SEE PAGES 26, 28, 30, AND 32.
Courtesy: University of Nebraska-Lincoln

letter writing, and itinerant peddlers, block patterns traveled from area to area. In each region, a block might acquire a new name.

Structured patchwork designs emerged, including Nine-Patch, Irish Chain, Pinwheel, Sawtooth Star, and Flying Geese. These early patterns are the foundations for hundreds of block designs that followed.

Between 1840 and 1860 women made quilts to raise funds and make statements of friendship and social values. An important trend was the creative, elaborate floral appliqué that began in Maryland and Pennsylvania. Most appliqué album quilts were samples of varied block designs, whereas patchwork album quilts usually featured the same block made from different fabrics. The appliqué quilts made in and around

STARS QUILT
c. 1850s

MULTICOLOR SOLID AND PLAID SILKS ARE HAND-PIECED WITH BEIGE SILK TO FORM 8-POINTED STARS ON THIS QUILT. A GREEN SILK SWAG AND PINK BUDS FRAME THE STARS AND SETTING BLOCKS. FULL INSTRUCTIONS ARE NOT AVAILABLE FOR THIS QUILT. FOR THE BLOCK INSPIRED BY THIS QUILT, SEE PAGE 16. *Courtesy: University of Nebraska-Lincoln*

A PIECE OF QUILTING HISTORY

An early appliqué technique, broderie perse (Persian embroidery), called for foliage, flower, and bird motifs to be cut out and sewn with tiny stitches in this manner: "Stretch your background upon a frame, and paste the chintz flowers into position upon it. When the pasting is finished and dry, take the work out of the frame and stitch loosely with as little visibility as possible, all around the leaves and flowers."

—FROM THE DICTIONARY OF NEEDLEWORK, 1882 EDITION

CRISS-CROSS QUILT
c.1855

RED AND WHITE WAS A FAVORITE COLOR COMBINATION USED IN QUILTS DURING THE MID-1800S. THE BACKGROUND FABRIC OF THIS QUILT IS A TINY BLACK-ON-WHITE PRINT. THE QUILT WAS PROBABLY MADE IN IOWA DURING THE 1850S. FOR COMPLETE INSTRUCTIONS TO MAKE THIS QUILT AS SHOWN, SEE PAGE 56. FOR THE 9-INCH BLOCK INSPIRED BY THIS QUILT, SEE PAGE 54.

Courtesy: Maryanne Lanigan

**FLYING GEESE
VARIATION QUILT**
c.1855

THIS FLYING GEESE VARIATION
USES RED-AND-WHITE BLOCKS SET
WITH WHITE SASHING. THE TURKEY
RED PRINTS ARE OVERDYED WITH
BLACK AND YELLOW. FOR COMPLETE
INSTRUCTIONS TO MAKE THIS QUILT
AS SHOWN, SEE PAGE 57. FOR THE
9-INCH BLOCK INSPIRED BY THIS
QUILT, TURN TO PAGE 52.
Courtesy: Ardith Field

1830-1860 continued

Baltimore between 1846 and 1860 were the height of this fashion. Baltimore album quilts were mostly appliquéd, and the women who made them strove to outdo one another with elaborate creations of bouquets, wreaths, and cornucopias. Too time-consuming to be practical for a utilitarian quilt, appliqué quilts were the pastime of a lady of leisure.

The diversity of pieced patterns continued to grow. Stars sprouted feathered edges and triangles acquired curved corners. These designs showed off the new roller-printed cotton fabrics, available in smaller prints than the old-fashioned plate and woodblock prints.

In contrast to the ladies of leisure in the cities, pioneer wives who followed their husbands during the mid-1800s picked out the few essential possessions they could carry as they moved to settle new ground. Quilts could be justified as bedding used to cover cabin doors, to shield crops from locusts, and as shrouds to bury the dead. Many women found the pioneer experience a desperately lonely life. The social and aesthetic values of quiltmaking offered solace as they dealt with isolation. Young girls learned to sew so they could help produce and mend the family

SHIPS OF MAINE QUILT
c.1845

FROM PENNSYLVANIA COMES THIS STUNNING INDIGO PRINT ON WHITE QUILT. THE HAND-PIECED QUILT EXHIBITS A STYLIZED SHIP WITH AN OCEAN WAVE BORDER. FULL INSTRUCTIONS ARE NOT AVAILABLE FOR THIS QUILT. FOR THE BLOCK AND BORDER INSPIRED BY THIS QUILT, SEE PAGES 18 AND 204.
Courtesy: University of Nebraska-Lincoln

A PIECE OF QUILTING HISTORY

A Long Island woman spoke of quilting with friends in 1826: "Clear and calm and very hot, the thermometer being as high as 108 — 4 persons sunstruck today and several yesterday...Sarah Baldwin, Frances and Jane Bergen, hear (sic) to help us quilt."
—JOHANNA BERGEN, KINGS COUNTY, LONG ISLAND, JUNE 11, 1826

FRIENDSHIP ALBUM QUILT
c.1853—1856

MADE BY MARGARET MORTON AND OTHERS IN PREBLE COUNTY, OHIO, THIS FRIENDSHIP ALBUM SAMPLER COMBINES PATCHWORK AND FINE APPLIQUÉD BLOCKS. THE DETAILED BLOCKS SET ON POINT TYPICALLY EMPLOY BRIGHTLY COLORED FABRICS ON A WHITE BACKGROUND. THE QUILTING IS UNUSUALLY FINE, WITH QUILTED NOSEGAYS IN THE SCALLOPED BORDERS. FULL INSTRUCTIONS ARE NOT AVAILABLE FOR THIS QUILT. FOR THE BLOCKS INSPIRED BY THIS QUILT, SEE PAGES 34 AND 36. *Courtesy: University of Nebraska-Lincoln*

ALBUM QUILT
c. 1850s

COMBINATIONS OF APPLIQUÉD MOTIFS ARE FEATURED ON THIS ALBUM QUILT FROM MARYLAND, INCLUDING A CHAIN OF CIRCLES, CONCENTRIC RINGS, AND A PINEAPPLE. THE TAN FABRIC THROUGHOUT THE QUILT WAS ORIGINALLY A DEEP GREEN, BUT THE DYE OFTEN FADED TO A DULL TAN AS SEEN IN THE VINES OF THE BORDER MOTIF—A CHARACTERISTIC OF GREEN TEXTILES OF THE PERIOD. FULL INSTRUCTIONS ARE NOT AVAILABLE FOR THIS QUILT. FOR THE BLOCKS INSPIRED BY THIS QUILT, SEE PAGES 42, 44, AND 46. FOR THE BORDER INSPIRED BY THIS QUILT, SEE PAGE 210.

Courtesy: University of Nebraska-Lincoln

bedding and clothing. By the age of 10 or 11, girls already had a few quilts to their credit. Whether the homes were in the city or along the new frontier, the quilts used and displayed in them brought comfort to the families who owned them.

THREE-PATTERN APPLIQUÉ QUILT
c. 1830

LOOK CLOSELY AND YOU'LL DISCOVER WHY THIS APPLIQUÉ SAMPLER IS CALLED THREE-PATTERN APPLIQUÉ. THE CREATIVE QUILTER USED HALF BLOCKS TO REACH THE OUTER EDGE. THIS SUMMER SPREAD WAS CREATED IN MONTGOMERY COUNTY, PENNSYLVANIA. FULL INSTRUCTIONS ARE NOT AVAILABLE FOR THIS QUILT. FOR THE BLOCK INSPIRED BY THIS QUILT, SEE PAGE 20.

Courtesy: University of Nebraska-Lincoln

A PIECE OF QUILTING HISTORY

"The patchwork bedcover was sewn to the quilting frames and suspended from the overhead beams by ropes attached at the four corners. Under this canopy was a fine playhouse for children, and many pricked fingers have resulted from bobbing heads beneath the quilt."

—HARRIET BONEBRIGHT-CLOSZ,
REMINISCENCES OF NEWCASTLE, IOWA, 1848

PERIOD FABRICS
1830–1860

AN ENGLISH IRONSTONE MILK
PITCHER DATED 1847 RESTS ON
BLUE, PALE YELLOW, AND RED
VINTAGE FABRICS. *Fabrics Courtesy: Ardith Field*

Fabrics Through Time

Although brown was a dependable color and often used in printed fabrics, quilts made in the mid-1800s were not drab—quite the contrary. Green and turkey red, which was often used with a white background, were the predominant colors. Unfortunately, some green dyes did not withstand the test of time. Fabrics treated with natural dyes retained green color; however, synthetic dyes developed in the late 1850s eventually became dull brown.

Turkey reds as well as indigo blue were favorites, partially due to their fade resistance. Turkey red, when used as background, was often overdyed with black, green, or yellow.

Rich Prussian blue was a favorite. Pinks were dark or soft and featured florals or paisleys. Double pinks appear in quilts dating in the 1840s and 1850s.

Yellow was used as a background and contained small black, red, or brown prints. Purples from this period are difficult to find because they often faded to brown. A permanent purple dye was not developed until 1862.

Linens and cottons were chosen instead of wool for their look and feel. Silk was sometimes used for coverlets on guest room beds.

Ombré print—fabric dyed with one color graded light to dark—was well-known from 1830 to 1850. This fabric was used to create an illusion of depth in appliqué quilts.

Simple plaids and light color backgrounds with large rows of prints were also popular.

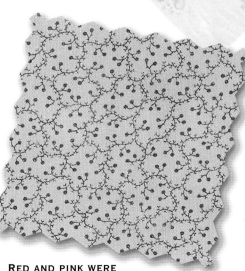

DEPENDABLE BROWNS WERE LIBERALLY USED DURING THE EARLY 1800S.

RED AND PINK WERE PRINTED ON WHITE BACKGROUND.

PASTEL PINK AND DARK RED WERE USED IN FLORAL PRINTS.

1830-1860 Silk Stars

These blocks are inspired by the antique quilt on page 8, bottom.

HOW TO CONSTRUCT THIS BLOCK

Sew A to A (4 times). Stitch two AA together (2 times). Sew the two units together. Sew B to B (2 times). Stitch two BB together. Machine-appliqué the star in place, matching the points with the background seam lines. Use matching threads to appliqué.

HOW TO MAKE THIS QUILT

This quilt is designed to be a full-size quilt measuring 90×90 inches, including 4½-inch sashing strips with setting squares and 9-inch borders with corner Star blocks.

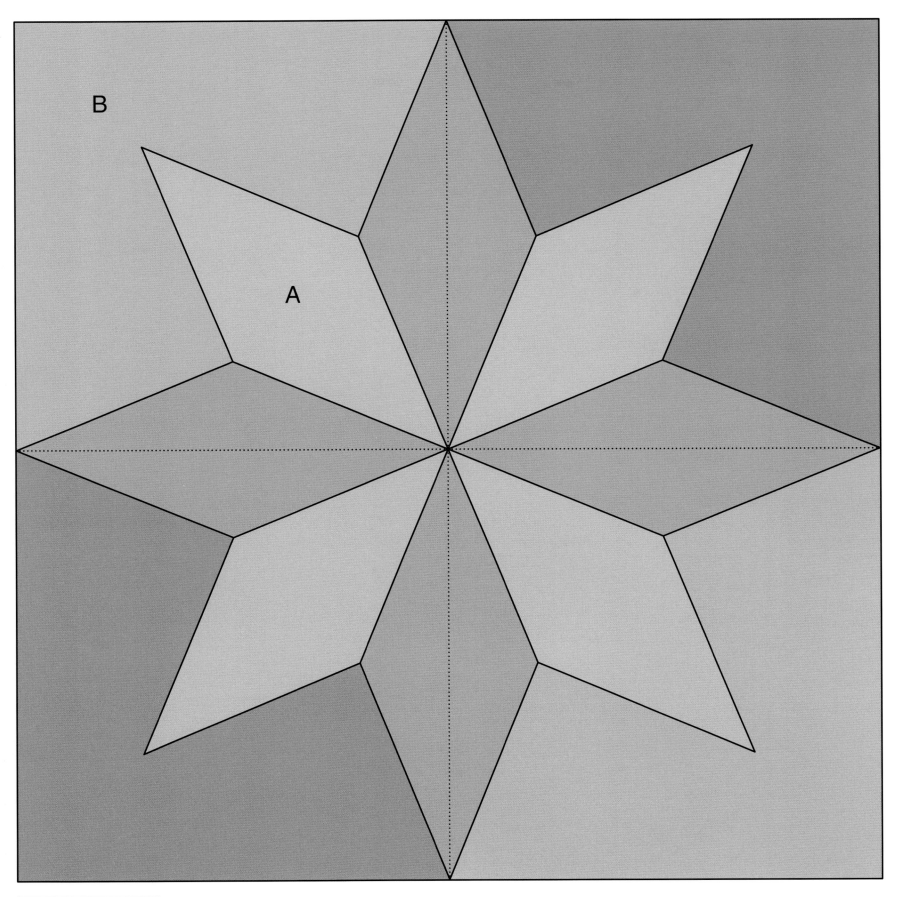

B

A

SILK STARS
full-size block

Ships of Maine Variation

These blocks are inspired by the antique quilt on page 11, top.

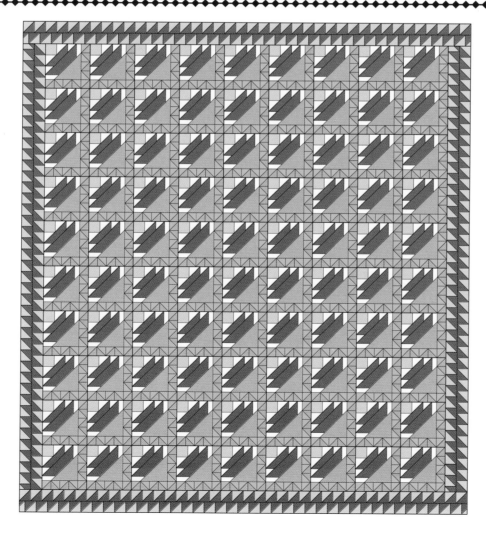

HOW TO CONSTRUCT THIS BLOCK

Sew B to A (2 times). Sew D to C (2 times). Stitch ABB to CDD. Sew F to E, add Fr. Sew ABBCDD to EFFr. Sew G to ABBCDDEFFr. Join two Hs (9 times). Sew four HH units together, noting color placement. Join to one side of ABBCDDEFFr. Sew five HH units together and stitch to the other side of unit.

HOW TO MAKE THIS QUILT

This quilt is designed to be a queen-size quilt measuring 90×99 inches, including a 4½-inch Zigzag border from *page 204*.

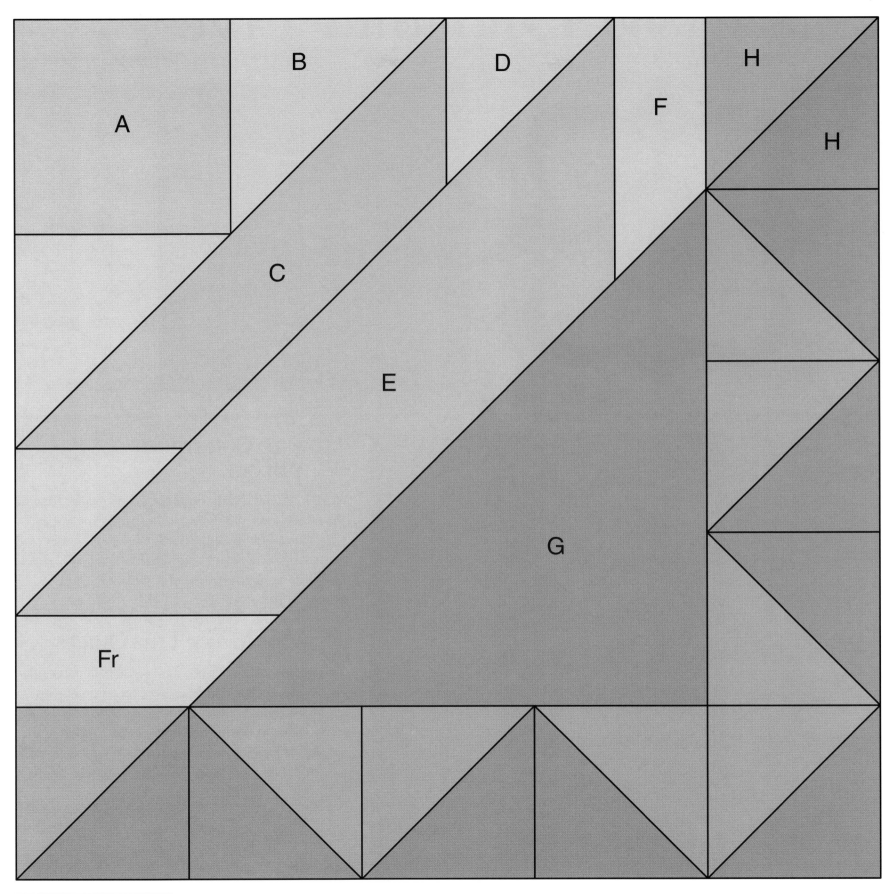

1830-1860 Diamond Five

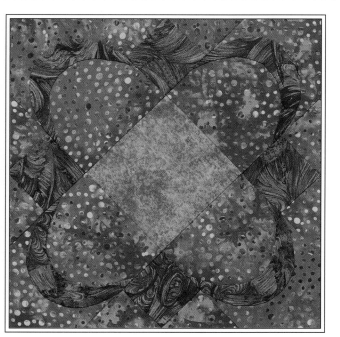

These blocks are inspired by the antique quilt on page 12, right.

How to Construct This Block

Mark B, C, and D with center guideline marks. To join the pieces, use a pin to match the marks. Stitch B to C (4 times). Add D (4 times). Stitch F to two sides of E (4 times). Sew EFF to opposite sides of BCD (2 times). Sew BCD to opposite sides of A. Stitch BCDEFF to opposite sides of ABCD.

How to Make This Quilt

This quilt is designed to be a twin-size quilt measuring 76½×103½ inches. The blocks are set on point with setting triangles bordering the blocks. The inner border is 2¾ inches at the top and bottom and 2 inches at the sides. The 4½-inch outer border is Diamond Link from *page 205.*

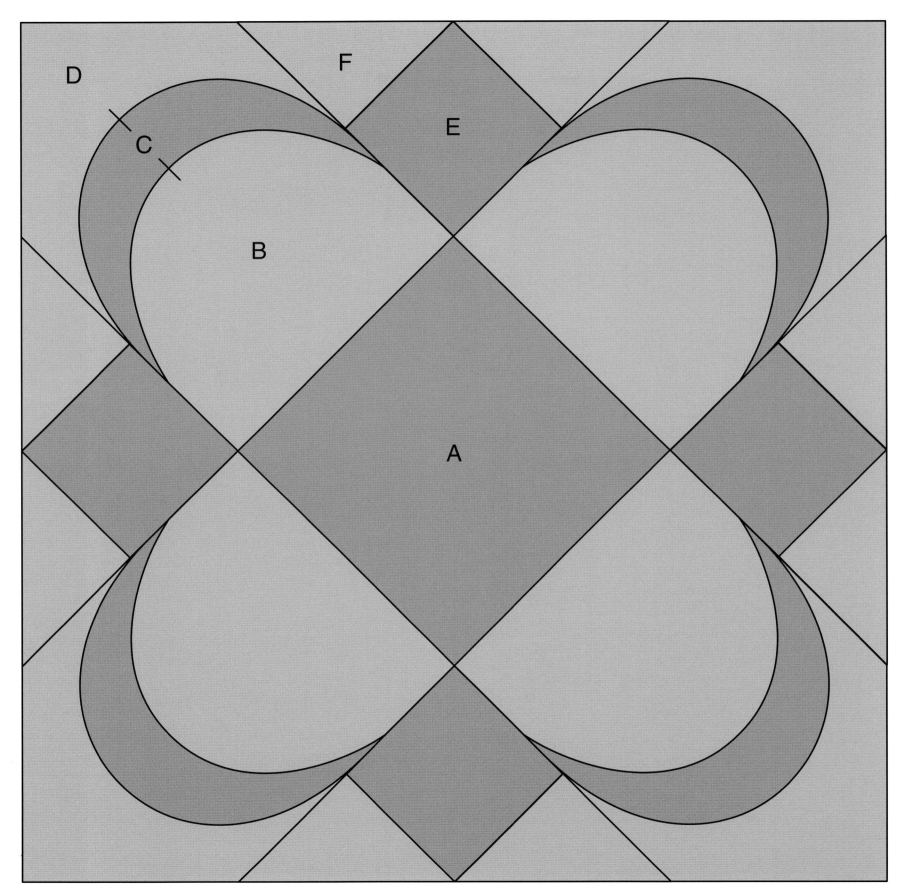

D

C

B

F

E

A

DIAMOND FIVE
full-size block

1830-1860 Geese in the Corner

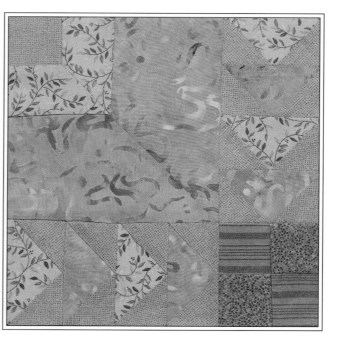

These blocks are inspired by the antique quilt on pages 6 and 7, bottom.

HOW TO CONSTRUCT THIS BLOCK

Sew B to C and Br to Cr. Sew BC to BrCr. Set in A to BC; stop the stitching at the seam line. Reposition A and begin stitching at the seam line. Be careful not to stitch through the BBr seam. Sew E to each short side of D (8 times). Stitch four EDE units together (2 times). Sew two Fs together (2 times). Join together to make a four-patch unit. Sew one EDE unit to the right side of ABrCr. Sew one EDE unit to the four-patch unit and join it to the bottom of the ABCEDE unit.

HOW TO MAKE THIS QUILT

This quilt is designed to be a king-size quilt measuring 93×114 inches, including 3-inch sashing strips with four-patch block corner squares. The plain inner border is 3 inches and the outer 3-inch Flying Geese border is taken from the block as shown.

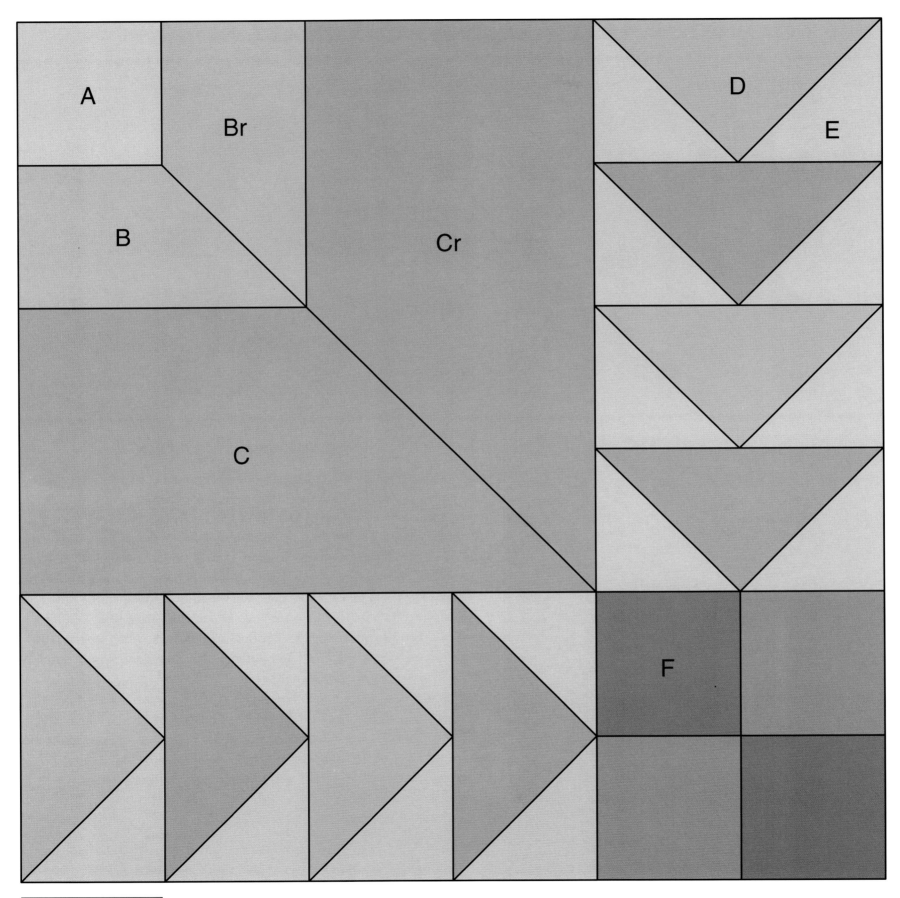

1830-1860 Mosaic Star

These blocks are inspired by the antique quilt on page 8, top.

HOW TO CONSTRUCT THIS BLOCK

Lay out pieces in correct positions, noting placement of half-square triangles for each CC unit. Sew A to Ar (4 times). Sew one long edge of C to A (4 times). Sew one long edge of C to Ar (4 times). Set in B to AArCC (4 times). Stop the stitching at the seam line of AAr. Reposition B and begin stitching at the seam line, being careful not to stitch through the AAr seam line. Sew two AArBC together (2 times). Stitch the two units together to form a center star.

Join C to C (24 times). Horizontally sew each row together. For Row 1 and Row 8: stitch two Bs, four CC units, two Bs. For Row 2 and Row 7: Stitch three Bs, two CC units, three Bs. For Row 3 and Row 6: Stitch separate row units—one CC unit and one B unit (4 times). For Row 4 and Row 5: Stitch two separate row units of two CC units each.

Sew one Row 3 unit to one Row 4 unit (2 times). Sew one Row 5 unit to one Row 6 unit (2 times). Sew the Row 3, 4 unit to the Row 5, 6 unit (2 times). Stitch one Row 3, 4, 5, 6 to the left side of the star center and one to the right side of the star center. Stitch Row 1 to Row 2; join to the top of the star center. Stitch Row 7 to Row 8; join to the bottom of the star center.

HOW TO MAKE THIS QUILT

This quilt is designed to be a twin-size quilt measuring 72×90 inches. Four rows of triangle squares form the border, with stars from the center of the block set in each corner.

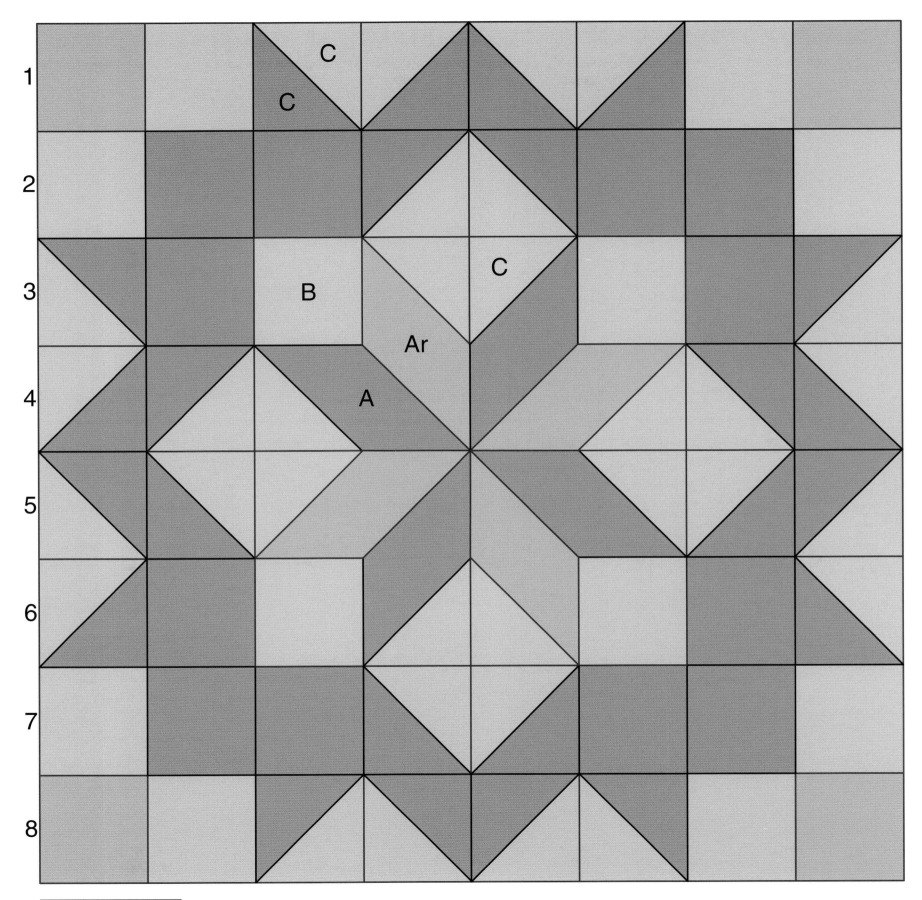

MOSAIC STAR
full-size block

1830-1860 Pinwheel Petal

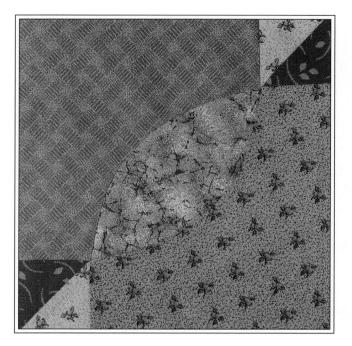

These blocks are inspired by the antique quilt on page 8, top.

HOW TO CONSTRUCT THIS BLOCK

Mark A and B with center guide marks. To join the pieces, use a pin to match the marks. Sew B to each side of A. Sew C to C (2 times). Set in CC to BAB (2 times), stopping the stitching at the seam line. Reposition CC and begin stitching at the seam line, being careful not to stitch through the BAB seam.

HOW TO MAKE THIS QUILT

This quilt is designed to be a queen-size quilt measuring 90×108 inches, including a border of 2×9-inch strips pieced together.

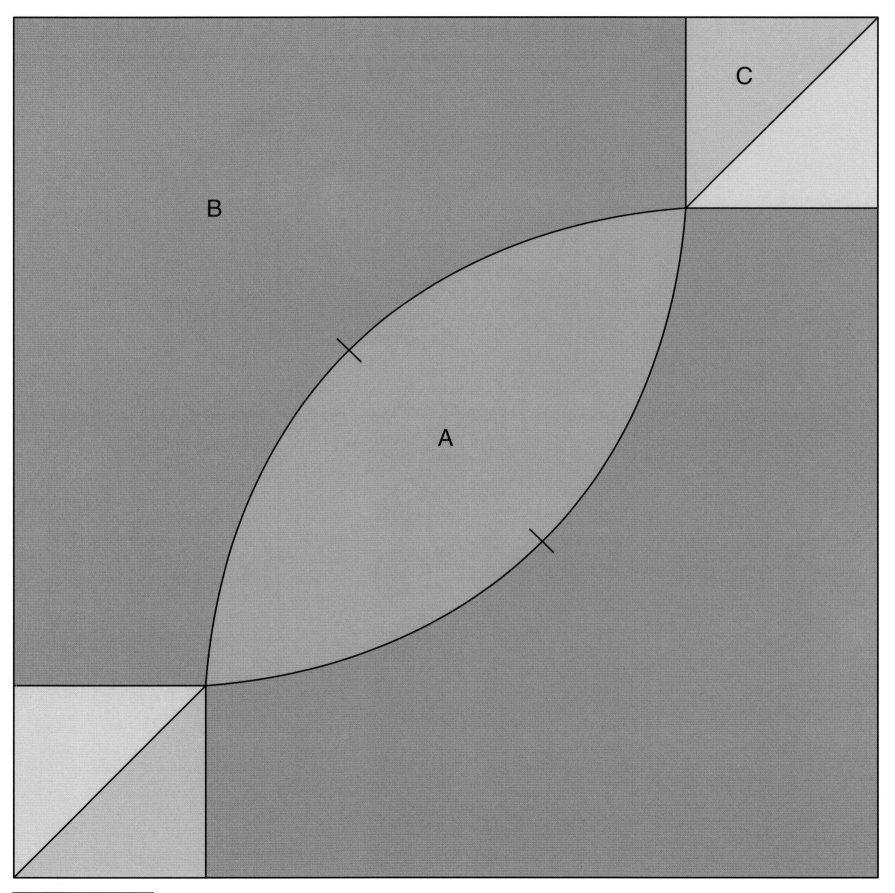

B

C

A

PINWHEEL PETAL
full-size block

1830-1860 Embroidered Basket

These blocks are inspired by the antique quilt on page 8, top.

How to Construct This Block

Sew A to B; add C. To ABC, add D. Sew G and Gr to ABCD. Sew E to F. Set in EF to ABCDGGr, stopping the stitching at the seam line. Reposition EF and begin stitching at the seam line, stopping the stitching at the next seam line. Reposition EF and begin stitching at the seam line. Appliqué I to H. Stitch IH to basket unit. Using the stitch diagrams on *page 199*, work stem stitches to embroider the flowers. Fill in the small berrylike flowers with satin stitches.

How to Make This Quilt

This quilt is designed to be a full-size quilt measuring 79½×92¼ inches, including 4⅞-inch inner border strips to frame the top and bottom of the basket block section and 7½-inch inner border strips at the sides. Setting triangles alternate with outer basket border blocks. An embroidered variation of the Starry Scallop border from *page 212* finishes the quilt.

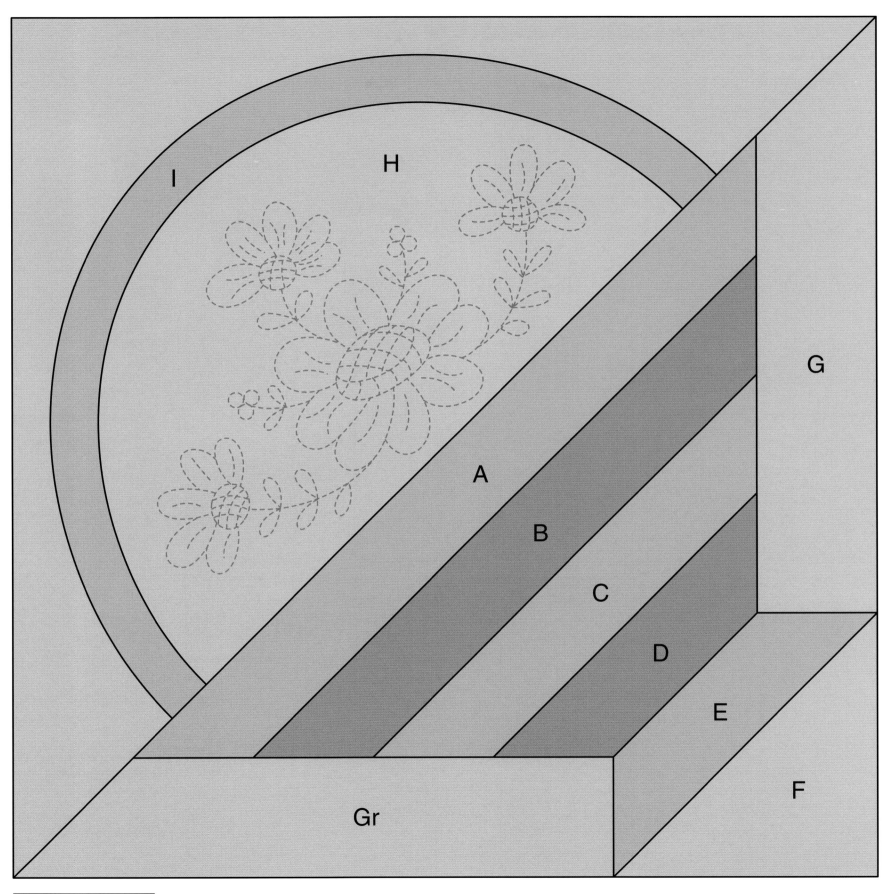

I

H

G

A

B

C

D

E

F

Gr

EMBROIDERED BASKET
full-size block

Carolina Lily Bouquet

These blocks are inspired by the antique quilt on page 8, top.

HOW TO CONSTRUCT THIS BLOCK

Unit 1: Sew A to Ar (2 times). Sew together the two AAr units. Set in B, stopping the stitching at the seam line. Reposition B and begin stitching at the seam line. Set in C (2 times). Sew D to ABC; add E to the one side. Sew F to ABCDE, completing Unit 1.

Unit 2: Sew G to Gr (4 times). Sew together two GGr units (2 times). Set in H to each set of GGrGGr (2 times). Set in I to each set of GGrGGrHH. Add J to each set of GGrGGrHHI (2 times). Sew K to L (2 times). Add Kr to KL (2 times). Sew KLKr to GGrGGrHHIJJ (2 times), making two of Unit 2. Sew Unit 1 to the left side of Unit 2 to make horizontal Row 1. Sew the right side of Unit 2 to square M to make horizontal Row 2. Sew Row 1 to Row 2. Make bias strips that measure 3/16-inch wide. Appliqué N, O, and P to each flower. Appliqué Q into a bow, adding R for a knot. In these blocks, the stems are braided and appliquéd to add dimension to the block.

HOW TO MAKE THIS QUILT

This quilt is designed to be a queen-size quilt measuring 90×108 inches, including three plain 4½-inch borders and two Spring Bloom borders from *page 208*.

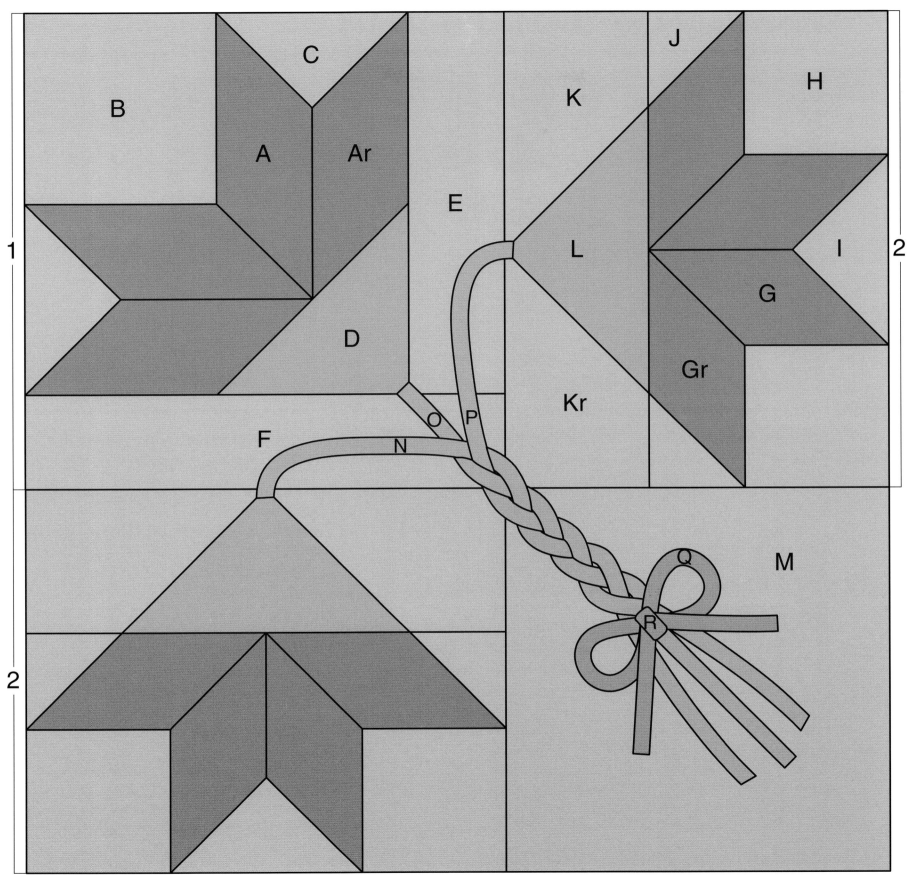

CAROLINA LILY BOUQUET
full-size block

1830-1860 Four Stars

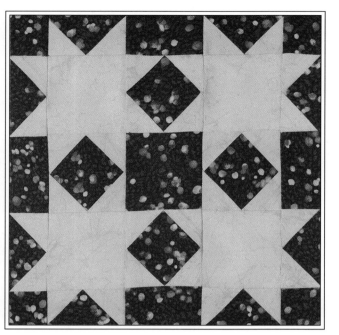

These blocks are inspired by the antique quilt on page 8, top.

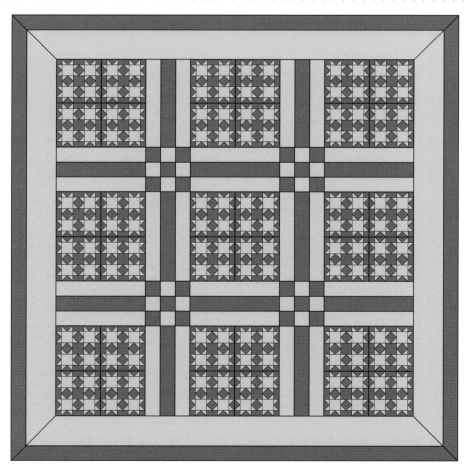

HOW TO CONSTRUCT THIS BLOCK

Unit 1: Sew B to A (8 times). Add B to the other side of A (8 times). Sew C to ABB (4 times). Sew ABB to outside edge of E (4 times). Add ABBC to adjoining outside edge of EABB to complete four of Unit 1.

Unit 2: To opposite sides of G, add F (8 times). To the remaining opposite sides of FFG, add F (8 times). Sew D to FFFFG (4 times) to complete four of Unit 2. Horizontally sew each row together. Rows 1 and 3: Sew Unit 1, Unit 2, and Unit 1 together. Row 2: Sew Unit 2, E, and Unit 2 together. Stitch Row 1 to Row 2; add Row 3.

HOW TO MAKE THIS QUILT

This quilt is designed to be a full-size quilt measuring 90×90 inches, including 9-inch pieced sashing strips with four nine-patch setting squares (composed of 3-inch squares). The mitered inner border is 6 inches, and the outer border is 3 inches.

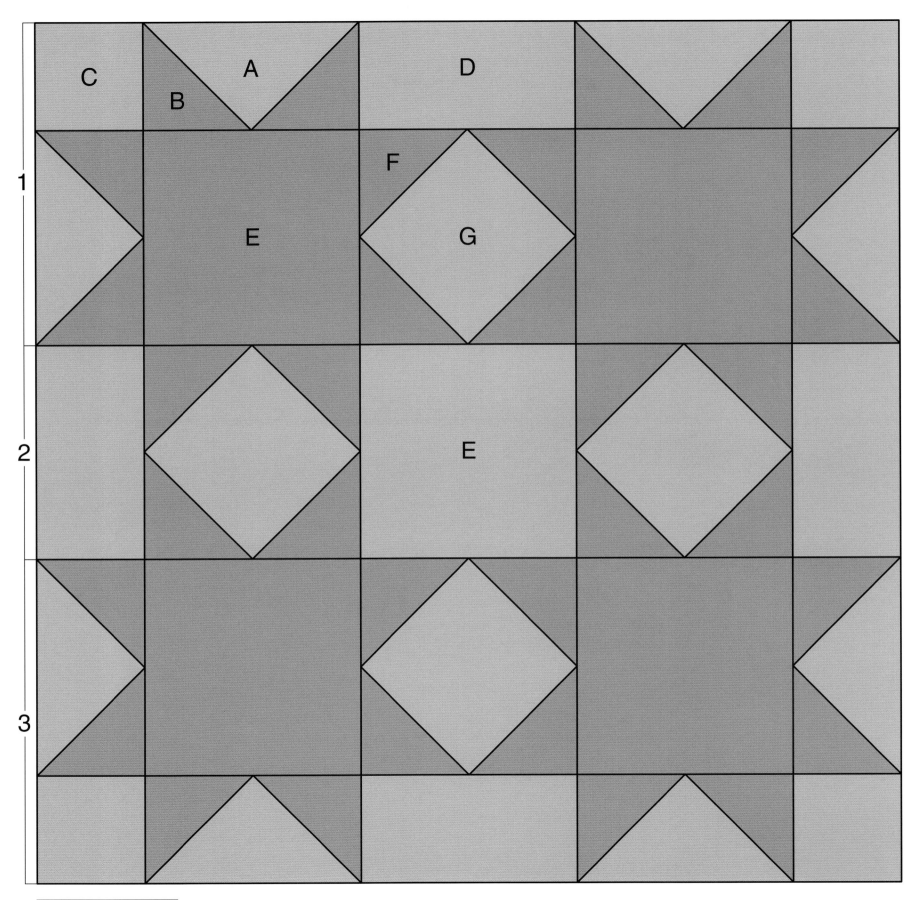

C
A
B
D
F
E
G
E
E

1
2
3

FOUR STARS
full-size block

1830-1860 Tulip Twist

These blocks are inspired by the antique quilt on page 11, bottom.

HOW TO CONSTRUCT THIS BLOCK

Fold a 10-inch background square in quarters; press. Beginning with A, arrange each piece. Appliqué pieces in place with matching threads. Trim block to 9½ inches square.

HOW TO MAKE THIS QUILT

This quilt is designed to be a twin- or full-size quilt measuring 81×99 inches. The quilt blocks are set with plain blocks. The 9-inch border combines appliqué from the quilt block with a variation of the Fancy Flower border from *page 210*.

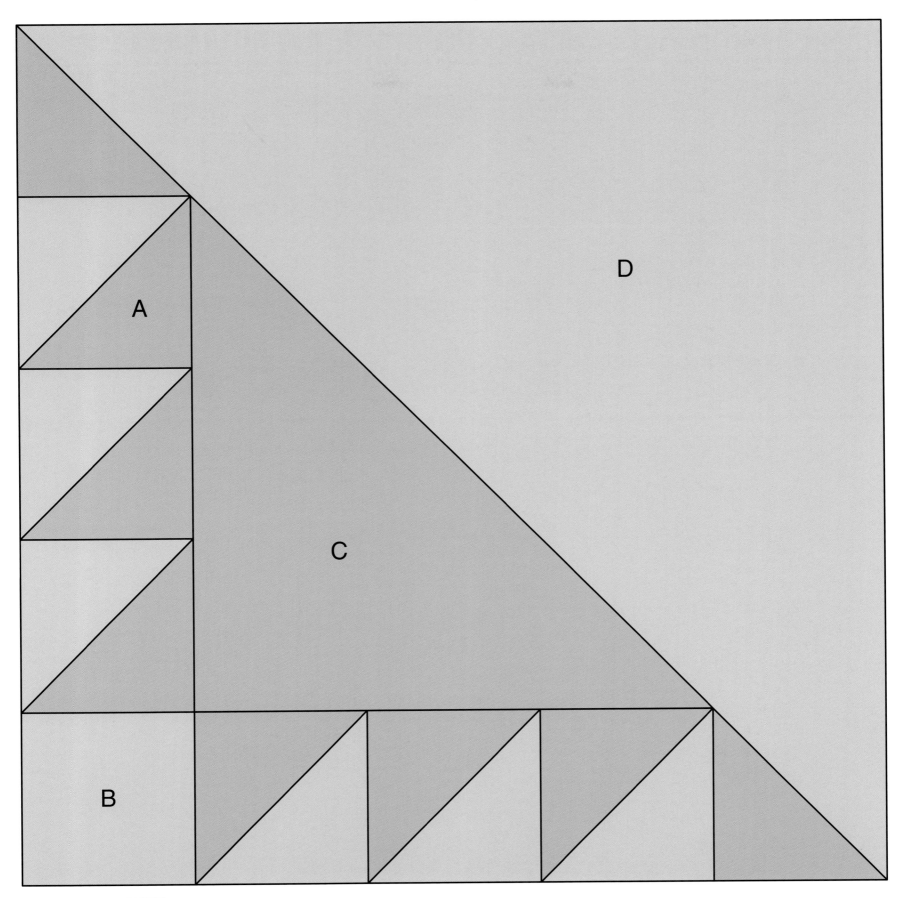

A

B

C

D

DELECTABLE MOUNTAINS
full-size block

These blocks are inspired by the antique quilt on pages 60 and 61, bottom.

HOW TO CONSTRUCT THIS BLOCK

Fold a 10-inch background square in quarters; lightly press. Arrange each piece on the square beginning with A. Appliqué all pieces in place with matching threads. Trim block to 9½ inches square.

HOW TO MAKE THIS QUILT

This quilt is designed to be a queen-size quilt measuring 99×108 inches with the top designed to wrap over head pillows. Four central blocks are outlined with 2¼-inch mitered borders, then a 4½-inch blue mitered inner border. The pink outer border is 4½ inches, the blue sides and bottom are 9 inches, and the top blue border is 18 inches.

A

B

C

FLORAL APPLIQUÉ
full-size block

1860-1890 Garden Daisy

These blocks are inspired by the antique quilt on pages 60 and 61, bottom.

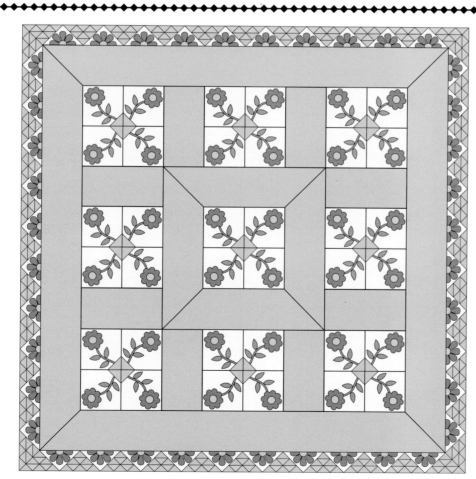

HOW TO CONSTRUCT THIS BLOCK

Position and appliqué E to B. Position all pieces in place on a 9½-inch background square and pin or baste. Appliqué all pieces in place, beginning with C, using matching threads. Sew A to bottom left corner over C.

HOW TO MAKE THIS QUILT

This quilt is designed to be a queen-size quilt measuring 99×99 inches. The center block is framed with mitered sashing, and 9×18-inch rectangles separate four-patch Garden Daisy blocks. The inner 9-inch border is mitered and a Daisy border, *page 207*, finishes the quilt.

A

B

C

D

E

GARDEN DAISY
full-size block

Floral Basket

HOW TO CONSTRUCT THIS BLOCK

Sew a light A to a dark A (9 times). Begin with the bottom left of the basket block. Row 1: Sew three A squares and one B square in a horizontal row. To the left side, add one A dark triangle. Row 2: Sew three A squares together. To the left side, add one A dark triangle. Row 3: Sew two A squares together. To the left side, add one A dark triangle. Row 4: Sew one dark A triangle to one A square. To the top of the A square, sew one dark A triangle. Sew Rows 1, 2, 3, and 4 together horizontally. Sew A to each short side of C (2 times). Sew ACA to Row 1 and stitch ACA to the opposite side of the basket. Add D. Lay the pieced basket triangle along E. Position the basket handle and stems to line up with the basket block. Appliqué with matching threads. Position the flower pieces, and appliqué beginning with stem pieces G, H, and I. Stitch the basket triangle to the appliquéd triangle.

HOW TO MAKE THIS QUILT

This quilt is designed to be a twin-size quilt measuring 76½×89¼ inches. Two 4½-inch inner borders with appliqué from the block create a central medallion. The outer setting triangles along the border are half basket blocks.

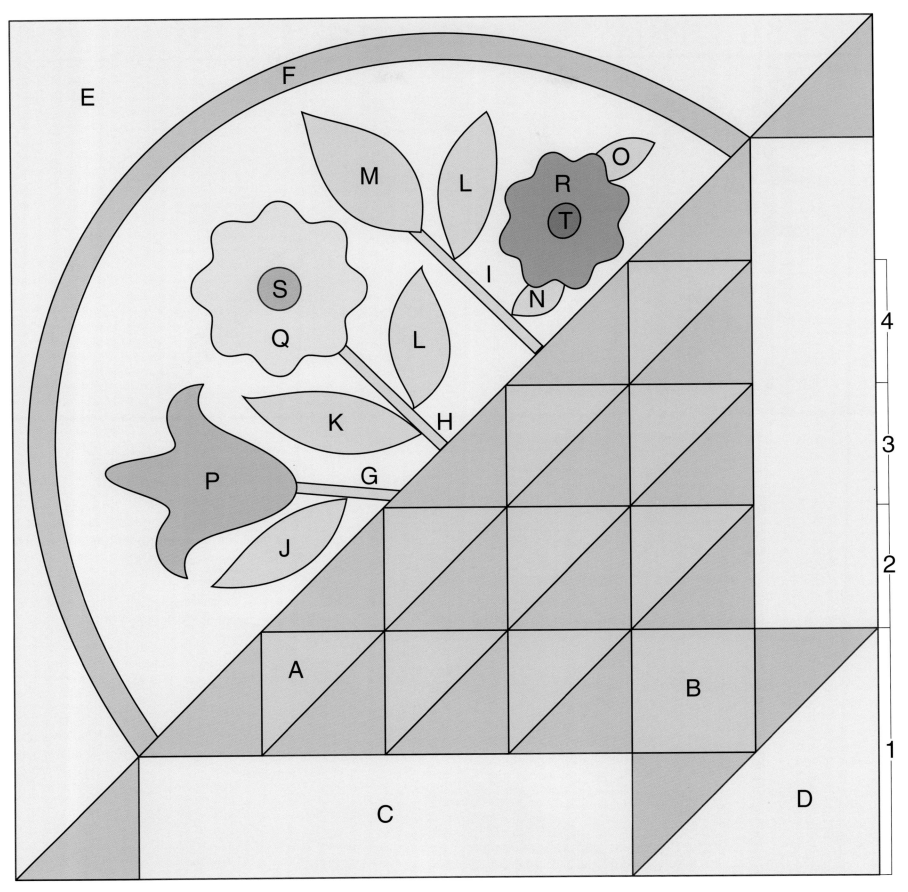

E

F

M

L

O

R
T

S

Q

I

N

L

K

H

P

G

J

A

B

C

D

4

3

2

1

1860-1890 Carolina Lily

 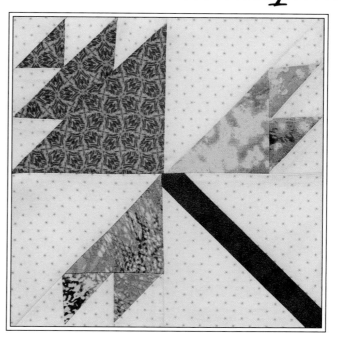

These blocks are inspired by the antique quilt on page 61, top.

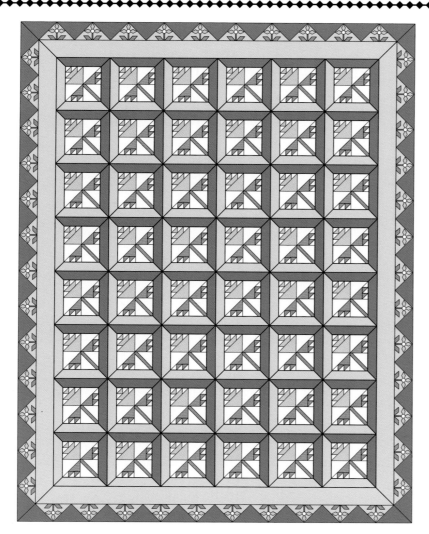

HOW TO CONSTRUCT THIS BLOCK

Unit 1: Sew A to A to make a square. Add A to each side of AA. Sew A to B (2 times). Sew AAAA to ABA. Add C.
Unit 2: Sew A to A to make a square (4 times). Sew AA to AA (2 times). Add A (2 times). Stitch AAAAA to D (2 times). Add C (2 times).
Unit 3: Sew E to each side of F.
Stitch Unit 1 to Unit 2. Stitch Unit 2 to Unit 3. Sew Unit 1-2 to Unit 2-3.

HOW TO MAKE THIS QUILT

This quilt is designed to be a queen-size quilt measuring 100½×120 inches, including 2⅜-inch mitered sashing, a 4½-inch mitered inner border, and a Spring Bloom outer border from *page 208*.

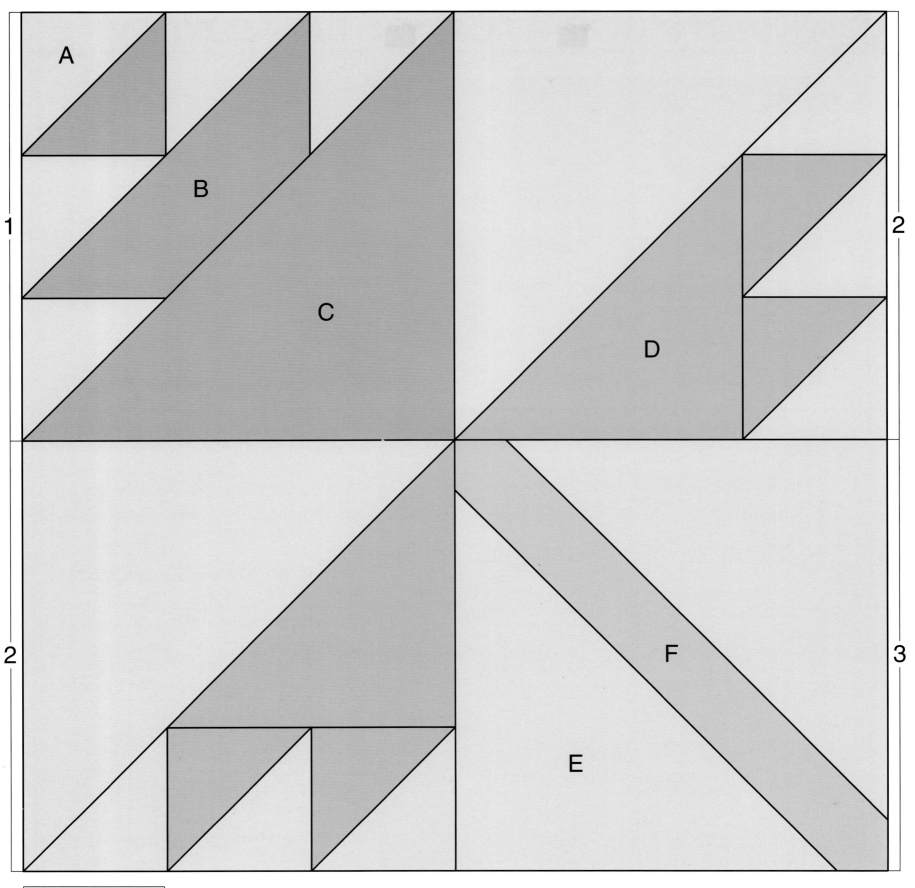

A

B

C

1

2

D

2

F

3

2

E

CAROLINA LILY
full-size block

79

These blocks are inspired by the antique quilt on page 66, bottom.

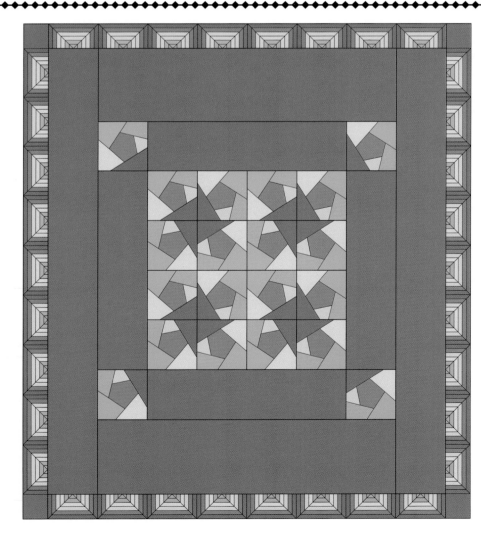

How to Construct This Block

Sew A to B. Sew C to AB. Sew D to ABC. Sew E to ABCD. Sew F to ABCDE. Using the stitch diagrams on *page 199,* add embroidery stitches to the block as desired.

How to Make This Quilt

This quilt is designed to be a twin- or full-size quilt measuring 81×90 inches and uses 9-inch strips with block corners for the inner border. The middle border has 9-inch sides and is 13½ inches on the top and bottom. The outer border is the Stripes Around border with plain corners from *page 206.*

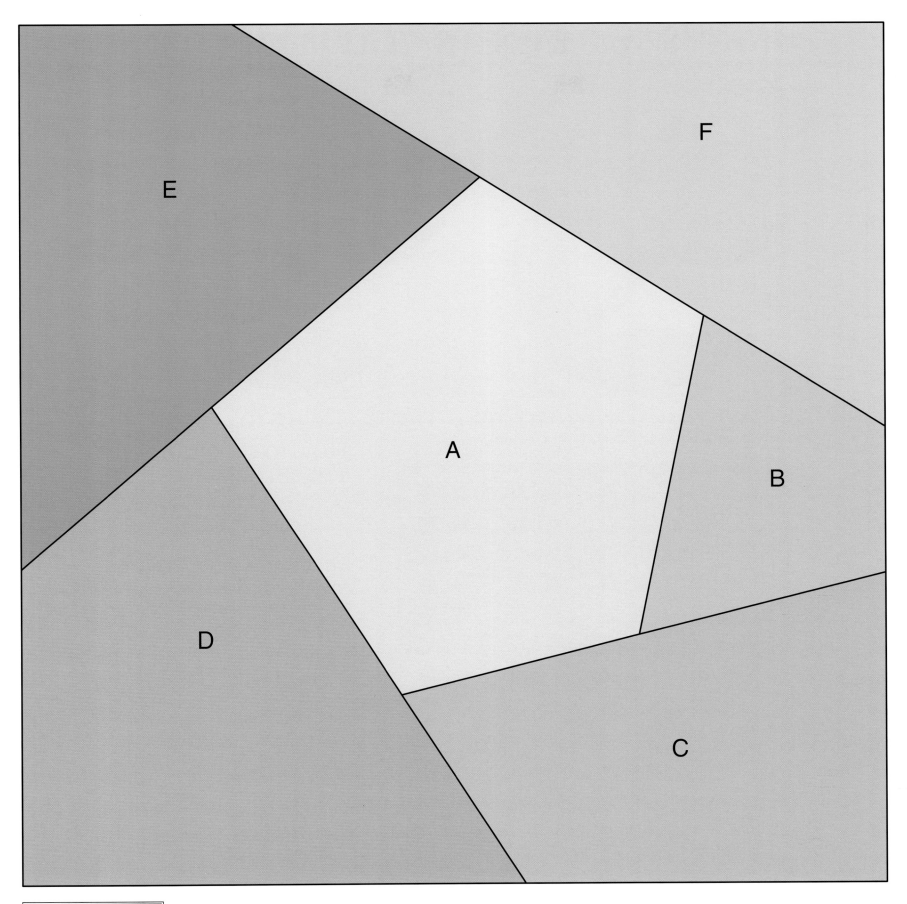

These blocks are inspired by the antique quilt on page 62, top.

HOW TO CONSTRUCT THIS BLOCK

Appliqué F to E, using matching thread. Sew G and Gr to two adjacent sides of EF. Sew H and Hr to remaining two adjacent sides of EFG. Stitch B to A (4 times). Fold AB background square diagonally once; press. Arrange each piece, beginning with C onto the background square. Appliqué all pieces in place with matching threads.

HOW TO MAKE THIS QUILT

This quilt is designed to be a full-size quilt measuring 81×99 inches, including 4½-inch borders.

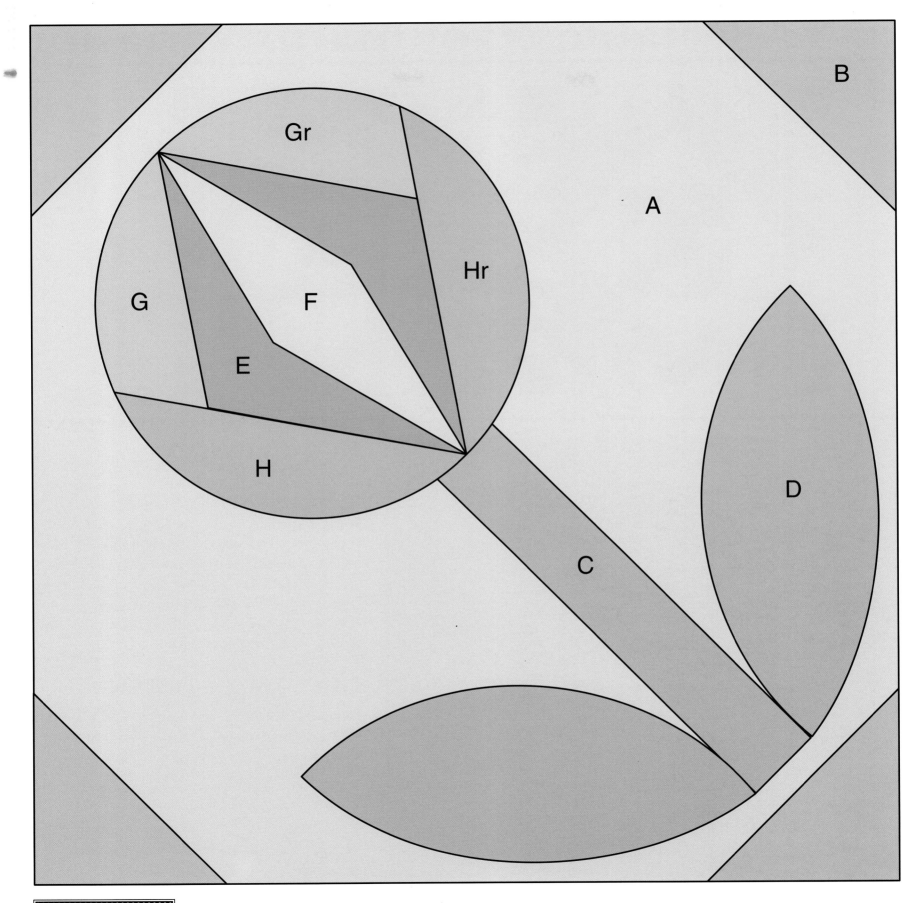

Gr

Hr

B

A

G

F

E

H

D

C

Delectable Mountains Variation

These blocks are inspired by the antique quilt on page 62, bottom.

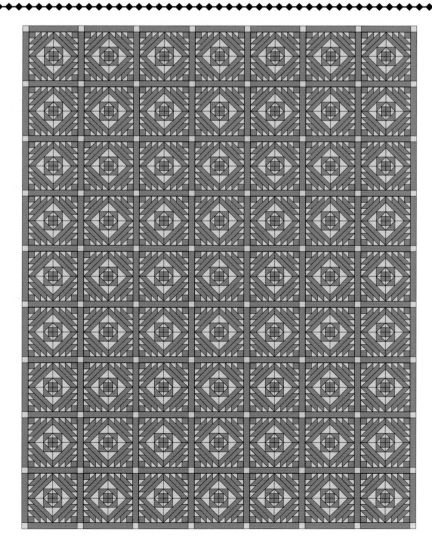

HOW TO CONSTRUCT THIS BLOCK

Sew A to two sides of B (4 times). Add C (4 times). Sew D to two sides of ABC (4 times). Sew E to ABCD (4 times). Sew F to two sides of G (4 times). Sew FG to ABCDE (4 times). Sew F to two sides of H (4 times). Sew FH to ABCDEFG (4 times). Sew F to two sides of I (4 times). Sew FI to ABCDEFGFH (4 times) to make four units. Sew two units together (2 times). Stitch the two rows together to complete the block.

HOW TO MAKE THIS QUILT

This quilt is designed to be a twin-size quilt measuring 72×92¼ inches, including 1⅛-inch sashing with setting squares.

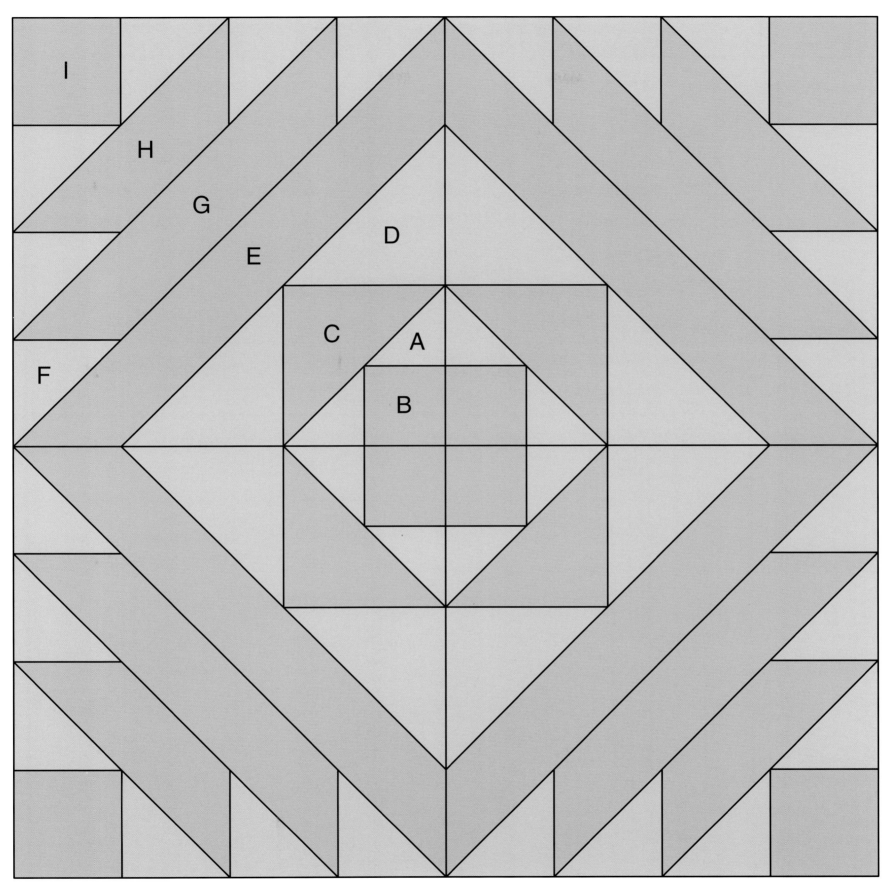

I

H

G

E

D

C

A

B

F

DELECTABLE MOUNTAINS VARIATION
full-size block

These blocks are inspired by the antique quilt on page 65, bottom.

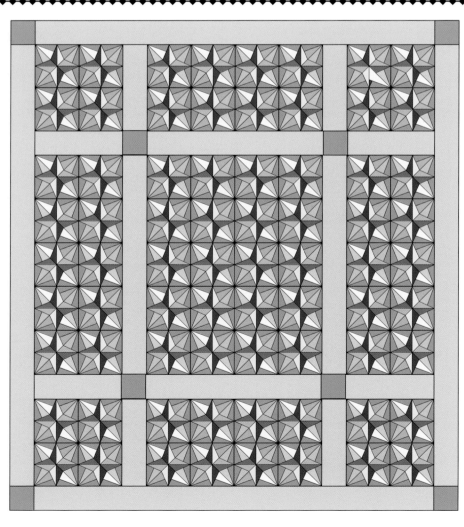

HOW TO CONSTRUCT THIS BLOCK

Sew A to B (4 times). Sew Ar to Br (4 times). Sew C to AB (4 times). Sew Cr to ArBr (4 times). Sew ABC to ArBrCr (4 times) to make four units. Stitch two units together (2 times). Join the units to complete the block.

HOW TO MAKE THIS QUILT

This quilt is designed to be a queen-size quilt measuring 90×99 inches. It includes 4½-inch sashing strips with setting squares. The border is a 4½-inch border with corner squares.

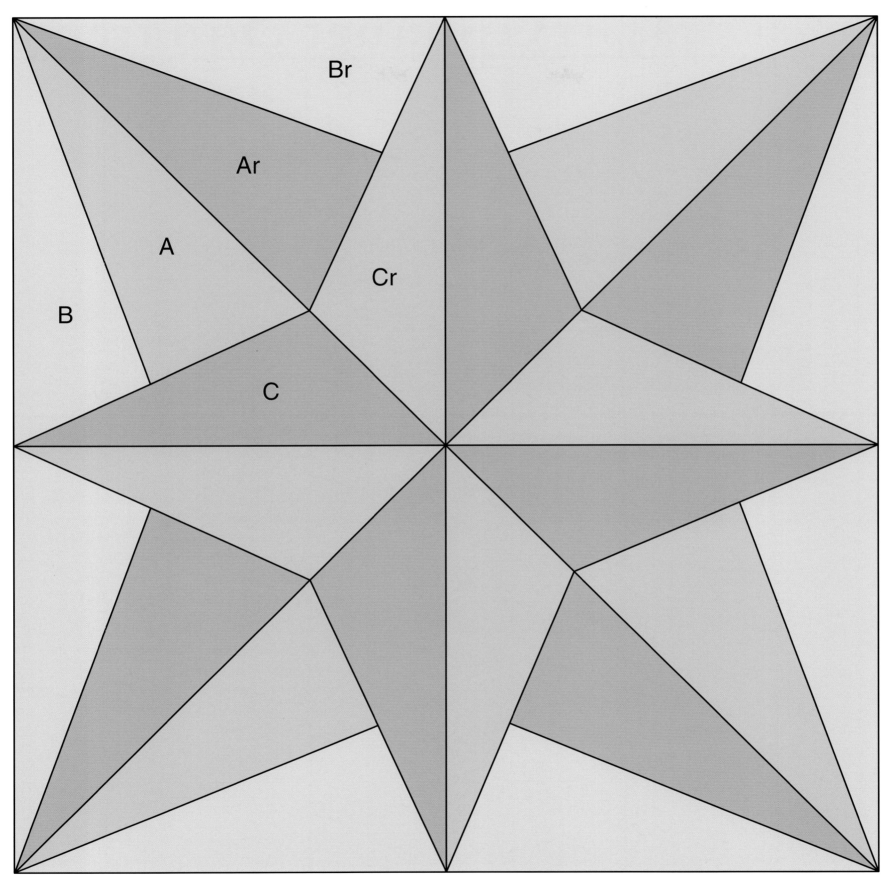

Br

Ar

A

Cr

B

C

STAR SHADOW
full-size block

1860-1890 Alphabet Square

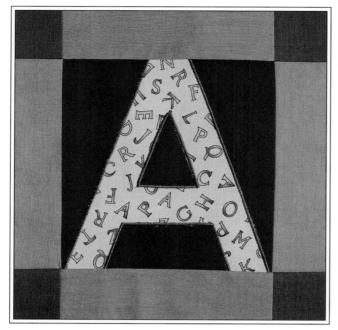

These blocks are inspired by the antique quilt on page 65, bottom.

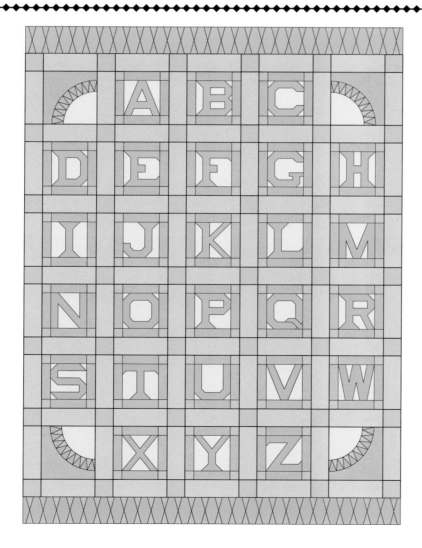

HOW TO CONSTRUCT THIS BLOCK

Appliqué B to the A square using matching threads. Sew D to opposite sides of A. Sew C to opposite sides of D (2 times). Sew CDC to the top and bottom of DAD. For the entire alphabet, see *page 213*.

HOW TO MAKE THIS QUILT

This quilt is designed to be a crib-size quilt measuring 58½×78¾ inches. The 2¼-inch sashing strips and setting squares separate letters, and New York Beauty blocks from *page 90* complete the corners. The top and bottom border is the Diamond border from *page 203*.

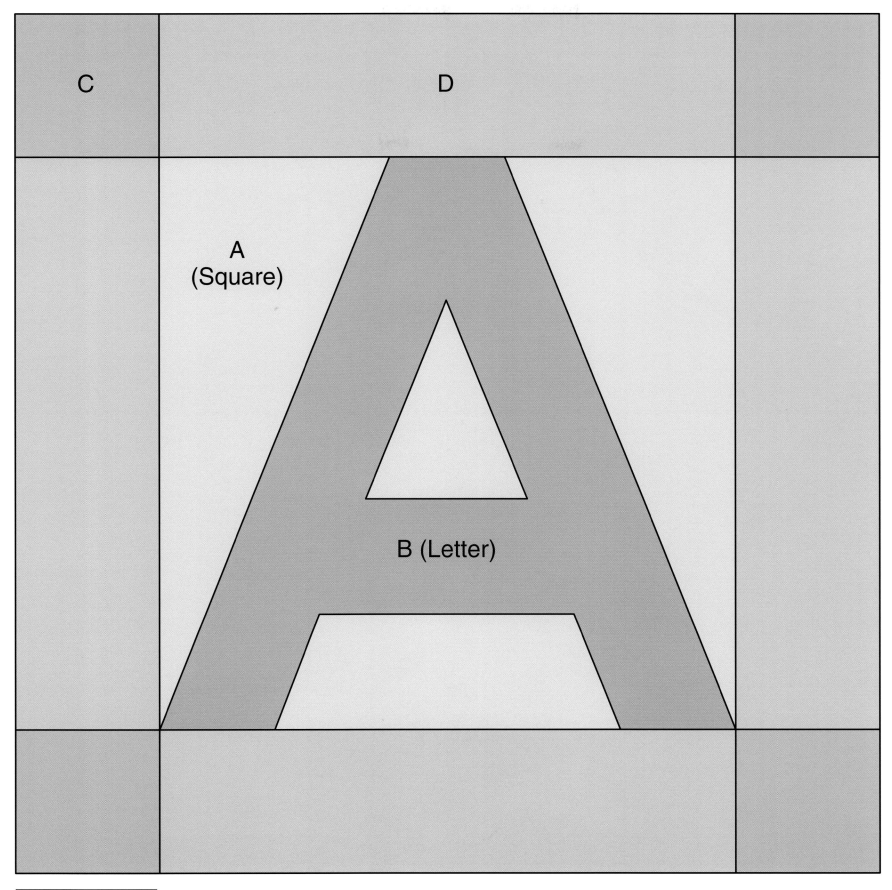

ALPHABET SQUARE
full-size block

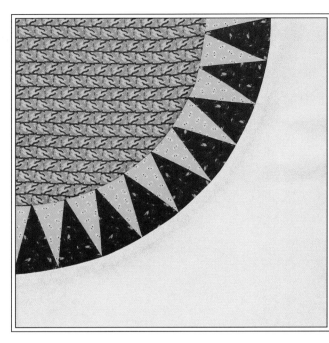

These blocks are inspired by the antique quilt on page 66, top.

HOW TO CONSTRUCT THIS BLOCK

Sew A to A (8 times). Sew AA to AA (4 times). Sew AAAA to AAAA (2 times). Stitch AAAA units together for a total of 16 As. Sew A to Br and stitch to the left side of unit A. Sew B to the right side of unit A. Pin at the dashed lines. Stitch C to AB unit, and ease in unit A to fit. Pin at the dashed lines and ease in fullness. Sew D to ABC unit.

HOW TO MAKE THIS QUILT

This quilt is designed to be a twin-size quilt measuring 81×81 inches, including the 4½-inch Sawtooth border from *page* 202 with corner squares.

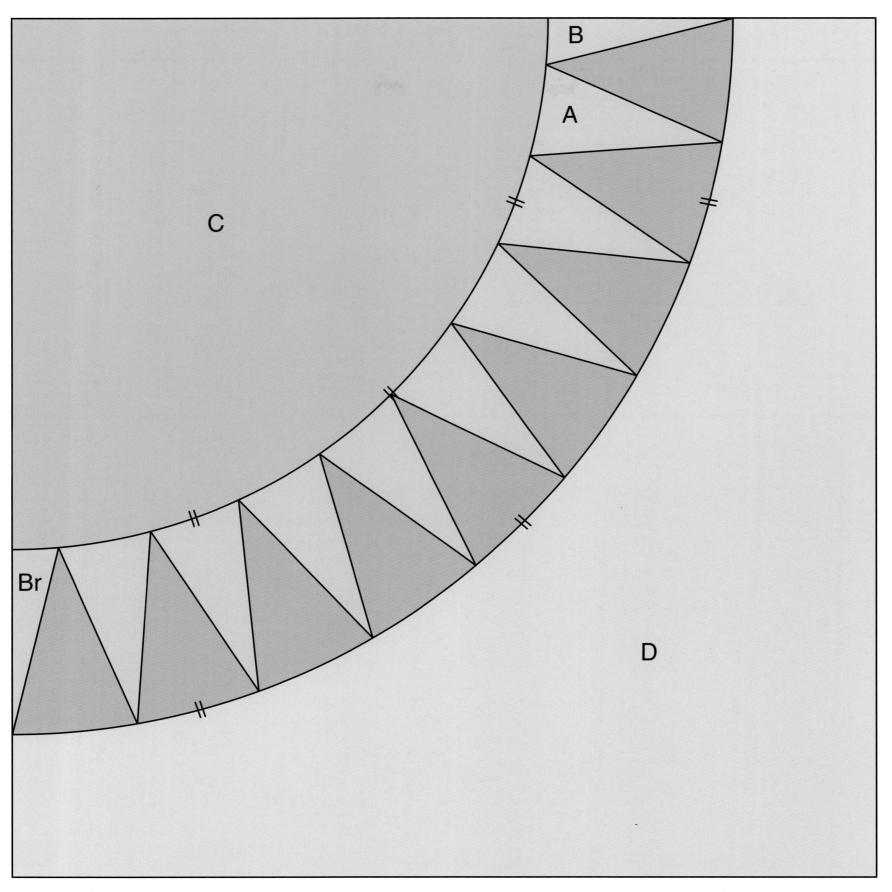

B

A

C

Br

D

These blocks are inspired by the antique quilt on page 63.

HOW TO CONSTRUCT THIS BLOCK

Sew a light A to a dark A (24 times). Sew AA to AA (8 times), add AA (8 times). Lay out a left and right diagonal row of the three AAA triangle squares (4 times), placing the light side of the squares in the correct position. Left Side Diagonal Row: Sew a dark A triangle to the top of AAA (4 times). Sew B to the left side of AAAA (4 times). Sew short side of C to the right side of AAAAB (4 times). Right Side Diagonal Row: Sew a dark A triangle to the top of AAA (4 times). Sew a short side of a light triangle A to the bottom of AAAA (4 times). Sew B to the right side of AAAAA (4 times). Stitch the right side to the left side to make an ABC unit. Sew D to each side of ABC unit (2 times) to make Row 1 and Row 3. Sew ABC to E; add ABC to make Row 2. Stitch Row 1 to Row 2. Add Row 3 to complete the block.

HOW TO MAKE THIS QUILT

This quilt is designed to be a full- or queen-size quilt measuring 93×93 inches, including 2½-inch sashing strips with setting squares. The inner border is 5 inches and the outer 2½-inch border is made from combining the star points on the quilt block (an ABC unit).

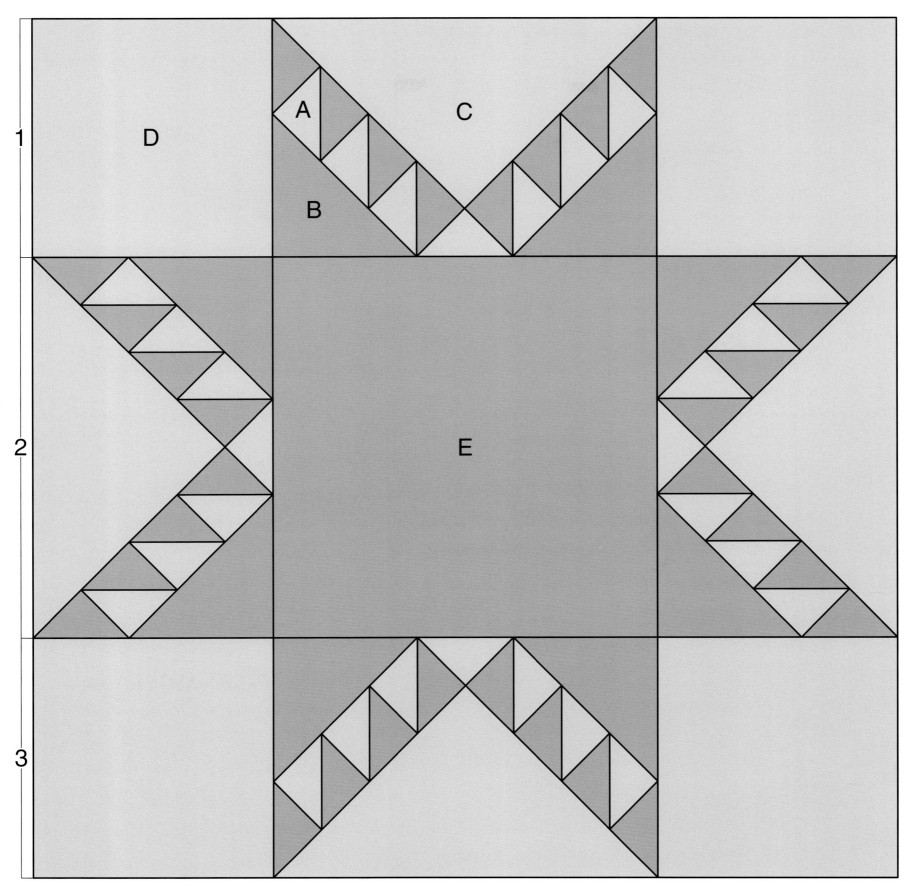

FEATHERED STAR
full-size block

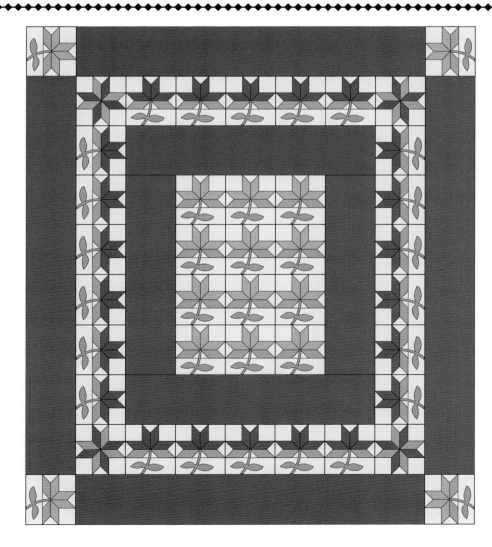

HOW TO CONSTRUCT THIS BLOCK

Sew medium A to background B; add medium Ar. Sew ABA to D. Appliqué E onto ABAD with matching thread. Sew a dark Ar to A (2 times). Sew ArA to ArA. Sew AAAA to ABADE. Set in triangle B to AAr (3 times). Stop the stitching at the seam line. Reposition B and begin stitching at the seam line. Be careful not to stitch through the AAr seam. Set in C (2 times), stopping the stitching at the seam line as above.

HOW TO MAKE THIS QUILT

This quilt is designed to be a full-size quilt measuring 81×90 inches, including 9-inch inner and outer borders with corner blocks. The corner blocks in the Peony block border use a variation of the block (using only pieces A, Ar, B, and C), creating a star motif.

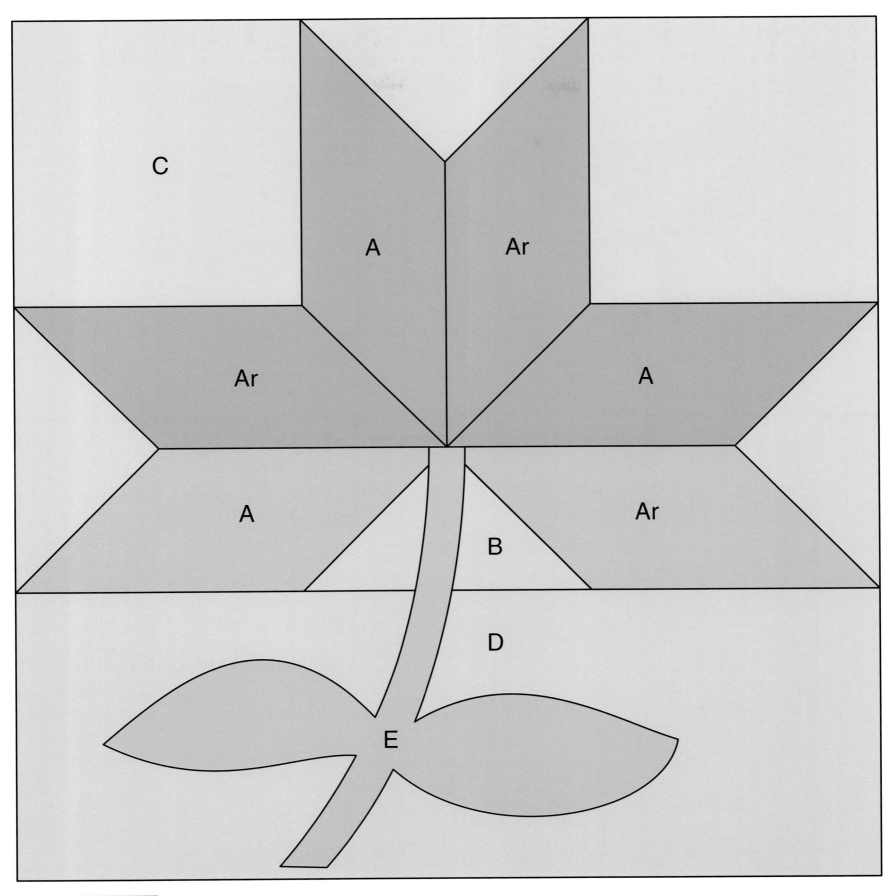

C

A   Ar

Ar   A

A   Ar

B

D

E

1860-1890 Colorado Block

These blocks are inspired by the antique quilt on page 64.

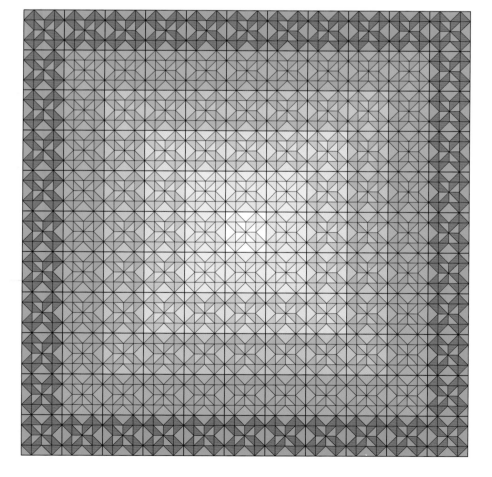

HOW TO CONSTRUCT THIS BLOCK

Sew light A to dark A (8 times). Sew dark A to each short side of B (4 times).

Center Unit: Sew AA to AA (2 times). Stitch AAAA to AAAA to make center block. Sew AA to ABA; add AA (2 times) to make Rows 1 and 3. Sew ABA to the left side of center block; add ABA to the right side of center block to make Row 2. Sew Row 1 to Row 2; add Row 3.

HOW TO MAKE THIS QUILT

This quilt is designed to be a queen-size quilt measuring 99×99 inches. White with light blue is used for the center block. Surrounding blocks are gradually darker, with the dark from the previous row becoming the light shade.

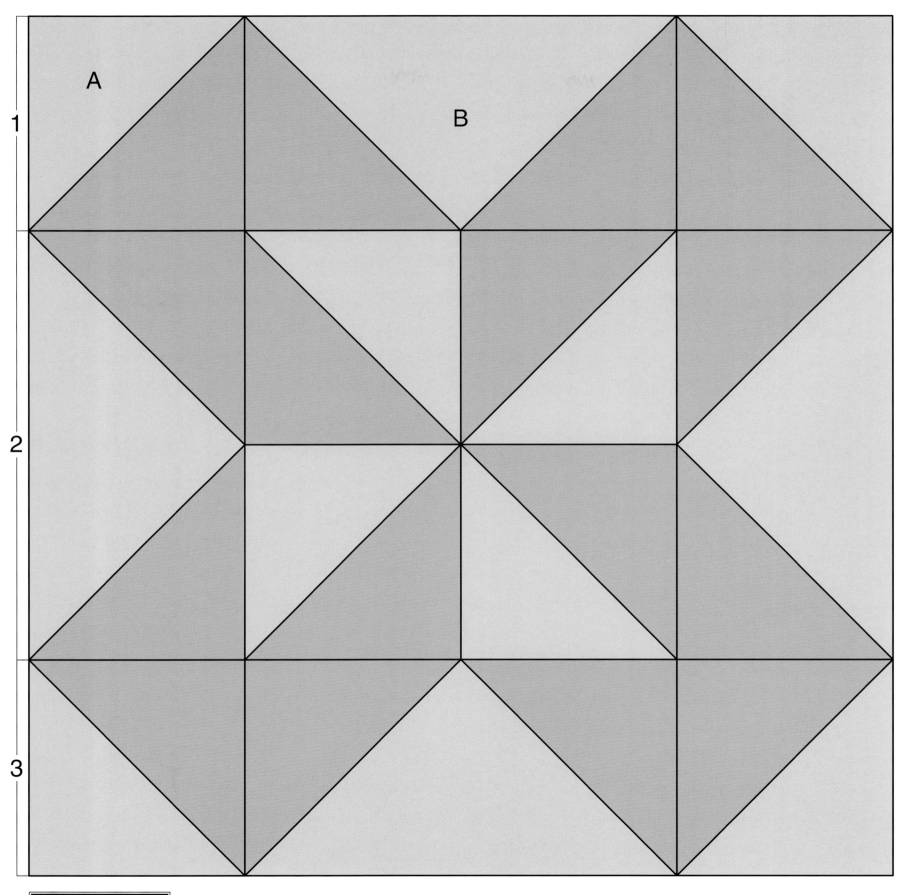

A

B

1

2

3

COLORADO BLOCK
full-size block

Quilt How-to

COLORADO BLOCK QUILT

Pictured on page 64.

MATERIALS

3 yards total of assorted prints
2½ yards of cream fabric for the block
    background
3 yards of dark print for setting blocks
    and binding
4 yards of backing fabric
72×84-inch piece of quilt batting

Finished quilt: 66×78 inches
Finished block: 6 inches square
    Quantities specified are for
44/45-inch-wide, 100 percent cotton
fabrics. All measurements include a ¼-inch
seam allowance unless otherwise specified.

CUT THE FABRIC

To make the best use of fabrics, cut the
    pieces in the following order.
    From assorted prints (you will need 8
    squares or 16 triangles from one print
    to complete a single block), **cut:**
    576—2⅜-inch squares, cutting each
    diagonally once to make 1,152
    triangles, or 1,152 of Pattern A
From cream fabric, cut:
72—4¼-inch squares, cutting each
    diagonally twice in an X for a total of
    288 quarter-square triangles, or 288 of
    Pattern B
288—2⅜-inch squares, cutting each
    diagonally once to make 576 triangles,
    or 576 of Pattern A
From dark print, cut:
71—6½-inch setting squares
8—2½×42-inch binding strips

MAKE THE BLOCKS

1. For one block you will need 16 same
   print A triangles, 8 cream A triangles,
   and 4 cream B triangles.
2. Follow the piecing directions on *page 96*
   to make 72 Colorado blocks.

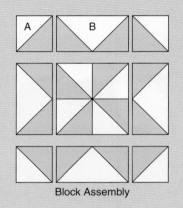

Block Assembly

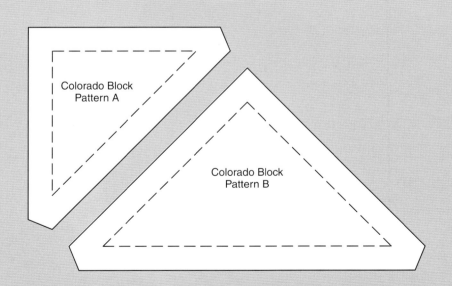

Colorado Block
Pattern A

Colorado Block
Pattern B

Quilt Assembly Diagram

ASSEMBLE THE QUILT TOP

1. Referring to the illustration, *above,* for placement, lay out 72 Colorado Blocks and 71 setting blocks in 13 horizontal rows with 11 blocks in each row. Sew the blocks together in each row. Press the seam allowances in one direction, alternating the direction with each row.

2. Join the rows. Press the seam allowances in one direction. The pieced quilt top should measure 66½×78½ inches, including seam allowances.

COMPLETE THE QUILT

1. Layer the quilt top, batting, and backing. Quilt as desired.

2. Bind the quilt using the dark print binding strips.

FEATHERED STAR QUILT

Pictured on page 63.

MATERIALS

5 yards of navy blue print
2¾ yards of white solid
4⅛ yards of backing fabric
74×86-inch piece of quilt batting

Finished quilt: 68×77¾ inches
Finished block: 13½ inches square
Finished half block: 6¾×13½ inches

Quantities specified are for 44/45-inch-wide, 100 percent cotton fabrics. All measurements include a ¼-inch seam allowance unless otherwise specified.

CUT THE FABRIC

To make the best use of fabrics, cut the pieces in the following order. The border and sashing strips are cut parallel to the selvage of the fabric. The listings include the mathematically correct border lengths. You may wish to add extra length to the borders to allow for any sewing differences. Trim the border strips to the actual length before adding them to the quilt top.

From navy blue print, cut:
2—3×78¼-inch border strips (#1)
2—3×63½-inch border strips (#2)
3—3½×73¼-inch sashing strips (#3)
16—3½×14-inch sashing strips (#4)
20—6½-inch squares, or 20 of Pattern E
72—3⅛-inch squares, cutting each once diagonally for 144 medium triangles, or 144 of Pattern B
144—2¾-inch squares, cutting each diagonally twice in an X for 576 small triangles, or 576 of Pattern A
8—2½×42-inch binding strips

From white solid, cut:
19—7¼-inch squares, cutting each diagonally twice in an X for 76 large triangles, or 76 of Pattern C
72—4¼-inch squares, or 72 of Pattern D
127—2¾-inch squares, cutting each diagonally twice in an X for 508 small triangles, or 508 of Pattern A

MAKE THE BLOCKS

1. For one Feathered Star block you will need 32 navy blue pattern A, 28 white pattern A, 8 navy blue pattern B, 4 white solid pattern C, 4 white solid pattern D, and 1 navy blue pattern E.

2. Follow the directions on *page 92* to make the 9-inch Feathered Star block. The completed Feathered Star block should measure 14 inches, including the seam allowances. Repeat to make 16 Feathered Star blocks.

continued on page 100

quilt how-to continued

MAKE THE HALF-BLOCKS

1. For one Feathered Star half-block you will need 16 navy blue pattern A, 15 white solid pattern A, 4 navy blue pattern B, 3 white solid pattern C, 2 white solid pattern D, and 1 navy blue pattern E.

2. Follow the directions given to make the 9-inch Feathered Star block on *page 92*, completing Rows 1 and 2. Trim the half-block to measure 7¼×14 inches, including seam allowances. Repeat to make 4 half-blocks.

ASSEMBLE THE QUILT CENTER

1. Sew a 3½×14-inch navy blue sashing strip (#4) to the bottom of 12 whole blocks and the 4 half blocks.

2. Lay out the blocks in four vertical rows, beginning with a half block and ending with a full block without sashing.

3. Join the blocks in each row. Press the seam allowances toward the sashing strips.

4. Lay out the four block rows and three long navy blue sashing strips. Join the rows to the sashing strips (#3). Press the seam allowances toward the long sashing strips.

ADD THE BORDERS

Sew a short navy blue border strip (#2) to the top and bottom of the quilt center. Join a long navy blue border strip (#1) to each side edge of the quilt center to complete the quilt top.

COMPLETE THE QUILT

1. Layer the quilt top, batting, and backing.

2. Quilt as desired. The original maker of the quilt quilted a diamond grid on the Feathered Star blocks and parallel grid lines on the sashing and borders.

3. Bind the quilt using the navy blue 2½-inch binding strips.

Feathered Star
Pattern E

Feathered Star
Pattern D

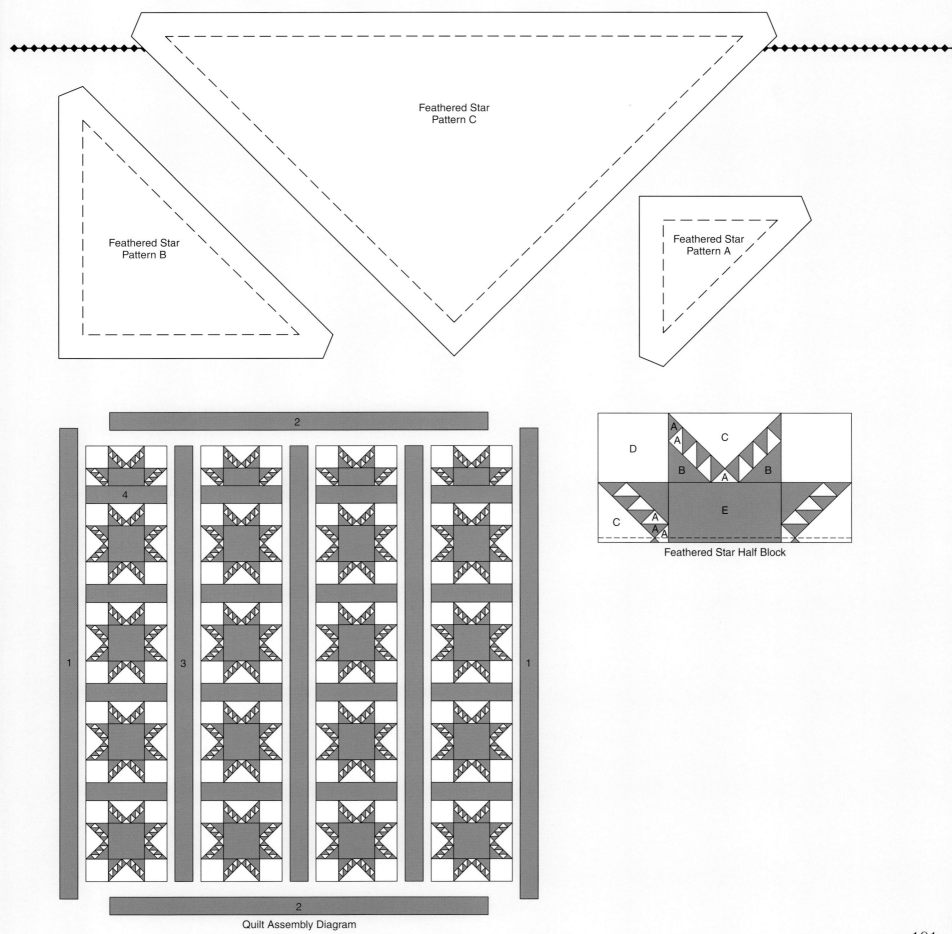

Feathered Star
Pattern C

Feathered Star
Pattern B

Feathered Star
Pattern A

D

A
A
C

B
A
B

C
A
E
A
A

Feathered Star Half Block

Quilt Assembly Diagram

Pieces of the Past from
1890-1920

From dark and somber fabric prints to graphic Amish masterpieces, this time period was a transition for the American quilter. Crazy, charm, log cabin, and pieced quilts continued to be popular during these years. The cheerier fabrics that would appear in the 1920s would come just in time for a new quilt revival. After the end of World War I the doors were opened for women, changing their lives forever.

Period Quilt History

Some dark and somber colors continued into the 1890s, and crazy quilting using silks and velvets continued. Interest in quilting began to fade a bit as most Victorians preferred to purchase ready-made bedding from the new Montgomery Ward and Sears Roebuck and Co. catalogs. This new method of buying products enabled affordable goods to reach even the most remote parts of the country. In the 1890 Ward's catalog, materials for a full-size quilt cost only $1.60, but wool blankets cost from $2.25 to $8.00. Relegated to make-do status for the poor, traditional quilts were denounced by fashionable magazines as common. Even magazines aimed at rural readers rarely offered quilt patterns until after 1900.

SAWTOOTH QUILT
c. 1890

MADE FROM A VIBRANT ARRAY OF SOLID AND PRINTED SILK FABRICS, THIS BEAUTIFUL QUILT IS MADE OF 10-INCH BLOCKS. THE INITIAL IN THE CENTER IS EMBROIDERED TO COMPLEMENT THE BLOCK. FULL INSTRUCTIONS ARE NOT AVAILABLE FOR THIS QUILT. FOR THE BLOCK INSPIRED BY THIS QUILT, SEE PAGE 118. *Courtesy: University of Nebraska-Lincoln*

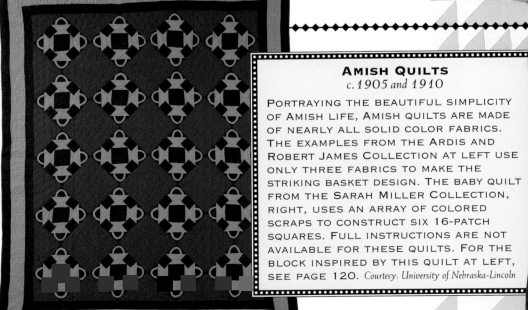

AMISH QUILTS
c. 1905 and 1910

PORTRAYING THE BEAUTIFUL SIMPLICITY OF AMISH LIFE, AMISH QUILTS ARE MADE OF NEARLY ALL SOLID COLOR FABRICS. THE EXAMPLES FROM THE ARDIS AND ROBERT JAMES COLLECTION AT LEFT USE ONLY THREE FABRICS TO MAKE THE STRIKING BASKET DESIGN. THE BABY QUILT FROM THE SARAH MILLER COLLECTION, RIGHT, USES AN ARRAY OF COLORED SCRAPS TO CONSTRUCT SIX 16-PATCH SQUARES. FULL INSTRUCTIONS ARE NOT AVAILABLE FOR THESE QUILTS. FOR THE BLOCK INSPIRED BY THIS QUILT AT LEFT, SEE PAGE 120. *Courtesy: University of Nebraska-Lincoln*

At the turn of the century, cheap manufactured products were readily available—quilts began to lose their popularity in American homes. Few appliqué quilts were made. However, pieced quilts continued to be made in rural areas.

Although the popularity of quilts waned in many cultures, Amish quilts kept the art form alive. Quilts made by the Amish women in the late 1800s and early 1900s were utilitarian, yet brilliant examples of rich vibrant color. The visually dramatic quilts are now hailed as works of art. Most Amish quilts are made of solid colors, often somber in tone and plain design.

TILE QUILT
c.1890

CONSTRUCTED IN BLOCK FORMAT, THIS UNUSUAL CRAZY QUILT HAS SHAPES SEWN ONTO A MUSLIN BACKGROUND, LEAVING NARROW OUTLINES AROUND EACH FABRIC PIECE AND BLOCK. INCLUDED ARE POPULAR VICTORIAN MOTIFS, SUCH AS MEN ON HORSEBACK, AN ELEPHANT, AND KITTENS. FULL INSTRUCTIONS ARE NOT AVAILABLE FOR THIS QUILT. FOR BLOCKS INSPIRED BY THIS QUILT, SEE PAGES 114 AND 116. *Courtesy: University of Nebraska-Lincoln*

CRAZY QUILT
c.1891

DATED FEBRUARY 17, 1891, THIS CRAZY QUILT FROM LANCASTER COUNTY, PENNSYLVANIA, COMES ALIVE WITH STRIKING RED AND BLUE EMBROIDERY. EACH FABRIC SHAPE IS OUTLINED WITH RED AND BLUE FEATHERSTITCHING, WHILE SATIN-STITCHED LEAVES, STARS, AND FLOWERS SEEM TO FLOAT AMONG THE CENTER BLOCKS. FULL INSTRUCTIONS ARE NOT AVAILABLE FOR THIS QUILT. FOR BLOCKS INSPIRED BY THIS QUILT, SEE PAGES 126 AND 128. *Courtesy: University of Nebraska-Lincoln*

A PIECE OF QUILTING HISTORY

"It took me more than 20 years, nearly 25, I reckon, in the evenings after supper when the children were all put to bed. My whole life is in that quilt... all my joys and all my sorrows are stitched into those little pieces. I tremble sometimes when I remember what that quilt knows about me."

—MARGUERITE ICKIS, QUOTING HER GREAT-GRANDMOTHER

GOOSE TRACKS QUILT
c. 1900

THIS BLOCK HAS SEVERAL NAMES—
PRIDE OF ITALY, THE CROSSROADS,
BLUE BIRDS FLYING, AND FANCY
FLOWERS—AS THE PLACEMENT
PROVIDES A VARIETY OF IMAGES.
FOR COMPLETE INSTRUCTIONS TO
MAKE THIS QUILT AS SHOWN, SEE
PAGE 142. FOR THE 9-INCH BLOCK
INSPIRED BY THIS QUILT, SEE
PAGE 140. *Courtesy: Living History Farms*

Amish quilts made in the United States before 1880 are generally dark blue, gray, brown, or black as a reflection of the society's rules that required dressing in somber tones and because of the small number of colorfast dyes available.

As colonies expanded beyond Pennsylvania—primarily Ohio, Indiana, Illinois, and Iowa—each settlement established guidelines for quilting. By 1890, Amish quilters expanded their color choices to include brighter options, though the prohibition against print fabrics remained universal. Quilts made in various parts of the country differed according to the rules of the Amish in that region. For example, quilts with lighter

SCHOOLHOUSE
c.1890

THIS BELOVED PATTERN EVOKES A NOSTALGIC IMAGE OF AMERICA'S ONE-ROOM SCHOOLS. THE PIECED BLOCKS ALTERNATE WITH STRIPED SETTING BLOCKS THAT RESEMBLE ROWS OF CROPS THAT SURROUNDED RURAL SCHOOLHOUSES. FULL INSTRUCTIONS ARE NOT AVAILABLE FOR THIS QUILT. FOR THE BLOCK INSPIRED BY THIS QUILT, SEE PAGE 112.
Courtesy: University of Nebraska-Lincoln

A PIECE OF QUILTING HISTORY

"I collected squares of calico— I liked assorting those little figured bits of cotton cloth, for they were scraps of gowns I had seen worn, and they reminded me of the persons who wore them."

—LUCY LARCOM,
A NEW ENGLAND GIRLHOOD

LOG CABIN
c.1890

CAREFUL PLACEMENT OF COLOR CREATES AN UNUSUAL PATTERN FOR THIS LOG CABIN QUILT. THE BRIGHT PINK CENTER CONTRASTS WITH THE CADET BLUE PRINTS THAT CREATE THE SERIES OF BOLD ZIGZAGS. FULL INSTRUCTIONS ARE NOT AVAILABLE FOR THIS QUILT. FOR THE BLOCK INSPIRED BY THIS QUILT, SEE PAGE 124. ANOTHER LOG CABIN QUILT IS ON PAGE 65.
Courtesy: University of Nebraska-Lincoln

MEMORIAL ALBUM QUILT
c.1914

MADE OF WHITE AND RED COTTON FABRICS, THIS QUILT IS PIECED AND APPLIQUÉD. THE CENTER MOTIF IS SIGNED "IN MEMORY OF J. BURTIS SCHOOLEY AND VIRGINIA W. SCHOOLEY. 1914." THE BORDER INCLUDES FIFTY 8-INCH BLOCKS, EACH WITH A SIGNATURE AND DATE. FULL INSTRUCTIONS ARE NOT AVAILABLE FOR THIS QUILT. FOR THE BLOCK INSPIRED BY THIS QUILT, SEE PAGE 122.

Courtesy: University of Nebraska-Lincoln

colors were most likely made in Ohio and Indiana; black and yellow tended to appear in quilts made in the Midwest. Even today, the strictest of Amish people still shun patchwork, believing that cutting fabric and sewing it together again is "just for pride." The borders are traditionally not mitered—it is less frugal to miter. Amish women often make quilts or quilt-pieced tops to sell to the outside world as a way of contributing to the family income. In these quilts you'll sometimes find calico prints not seen in the quilts they make for themselves.

By the end of WWI, the country was heading for prosperity and equality, and the 1920s would see changes in the American way of life.

SINGLE IRISH CHAIN
c.1890

THIS SINGLE IRISH CHAIN QUILT COMES FROM PITTSBURGH, PENNSYLVANIA. TINY HALF-INCH SQUARES, CAREFULLY PLACED, COMPOSE THIS ELEGANT AND GEOMETRIC QUILT. NINE-PATCH BLOCKS ON POINT ARE REPEATED IN THE OUTER BORDER OF THE QUILT. FULL INSTRUCTIONS ARE NOT AVAILABLE FOR THIS QUILT. FOR THE BLOCK INSPIRED BY THIS QUILT, SEE PAGE 130. *Courtesy: University of Nebraska-Lincoln*

A PIECE OF QUILTING HISTORY

"I've had a heap of comfort all my life making quilts, and now in my old age I wouldn't take a fortune for them."

—ELIZA CALVERT HALL,
AUNT JANE OF KENTUCKY 1898

O.N.T.

SPOOL COTTON

110

Fabrics Through Time

During the turn of the 20th century, fabrics reflected the colors of mourning. Empress Eugénie mourned her husband, Napoleon III. Queen Victoria mourned her husband, Albert, and her mother, the Duchess of Alba. It is thought that these deaths influenced the dreary colors of the time. People who mourned were expected to wear black clothing the first year after the death of a family member. After that, they might wear gray, dark purple, or dark blue.

In 1897, the Sears Roebuck catalog offered fabrics, including shirting prints, percales, sateens, and more. Mourning prints, listed in a separate category of importance, were phased out of the catalog within the next few years.

The available colors ranged from light blue and pink to Turkey red and Nile green. Faded reds, such as salmon pink, orange, and reddish brown were prominent in quilts around the United States.

These fabrics were possibly dyed with Georgia or Arkansas red clay.

Indigo blue prints were sometimes referred to as Dutch blue or German blue for countries known for skill in making blue dyes.

Another important blue in this era was cadet blue. This misty hue, often printed in combination with black or white, was vat-dyed to be equally blue on both sides of the fabric. In the early 1900s another blue was born, the color we now refer to as baby blue.

ROAD TO PARIS VARIATION
c.1890s

THIS ROAD TO PARIS VARIATION TYPIFIES EVERYDAY PATCHWORK THAT, BECAUSE OF ITS VISUAL SOPHISTICATION, HAS BEEN RECOGNIZED AS A SIGNIFICANT PART OF AMERICAN DESIGN. THE RICH INDIGO SASHING SEEMS TO ZIGZAG VERTICALLY BETWEEN THE BLOCKS, PRODUCING AN UNDULATING EFFECT. FULL INSTRUCTIONS ARE NOT AVAILABLE FOR THIS QUILT. FOR THE BLOCK INSPIRED BY THIS QUILT, SEE PAGE 132. *Courtesy: University of Nebraska-Lincoln*

INDIGO BLUE FABRICS WERE SOMETIMES OVERPRINTED WITH CHROME YELLOW.

THIS TINY BLACK PRINT SHIRTING FABRIC IS PRINTED ON A WHITE GROUND.

VIBRANT REDS OFTEN HAD ALLOVER PRINTS.

These blocks are inspired by the antique quilt on page 107, top.

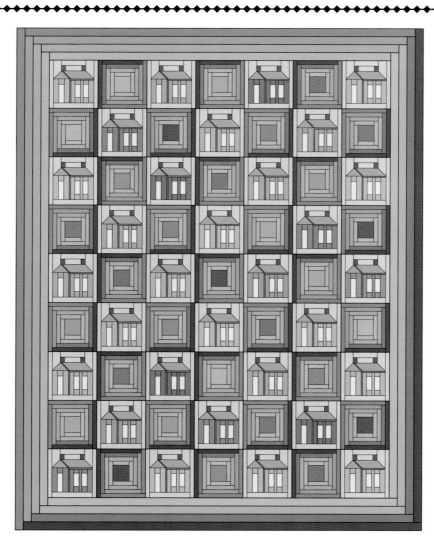

How to Construct This Block

This block will be constructed in three parts.

Unit 1: Sew B to each short side of A; add C. Sew E to D; add F. Stitch ABC to DEF. Set in G and Gr. Stop the stitching at the seam line of BF and BD. Reposition G and Gr and begin stitching at the seam line.

Unit 2: Sew H to I. Add J to each side of HI.

Unit 3: Sew B to the top of K (2 times). Sew H to the bottom of BK (2 times). Sew L to BKH; add BKH. Sew M to left side of BKHL; add J to right side. Sew N to the left edge of BKHLM; sew O to the top of BKHLMN. Sew Unit 2 to Unit 3. Add P to the bottom. Add Unit 1. Sew Q to the side edge of the house block (2 times).

How to Make This Quilt

This quilt is designed to be a twin-size quilt measuring 75×93 inches, including four 1½-inch borders. The Schoolhouse blocks alternate with Log Cabin blocks from *page 124*.

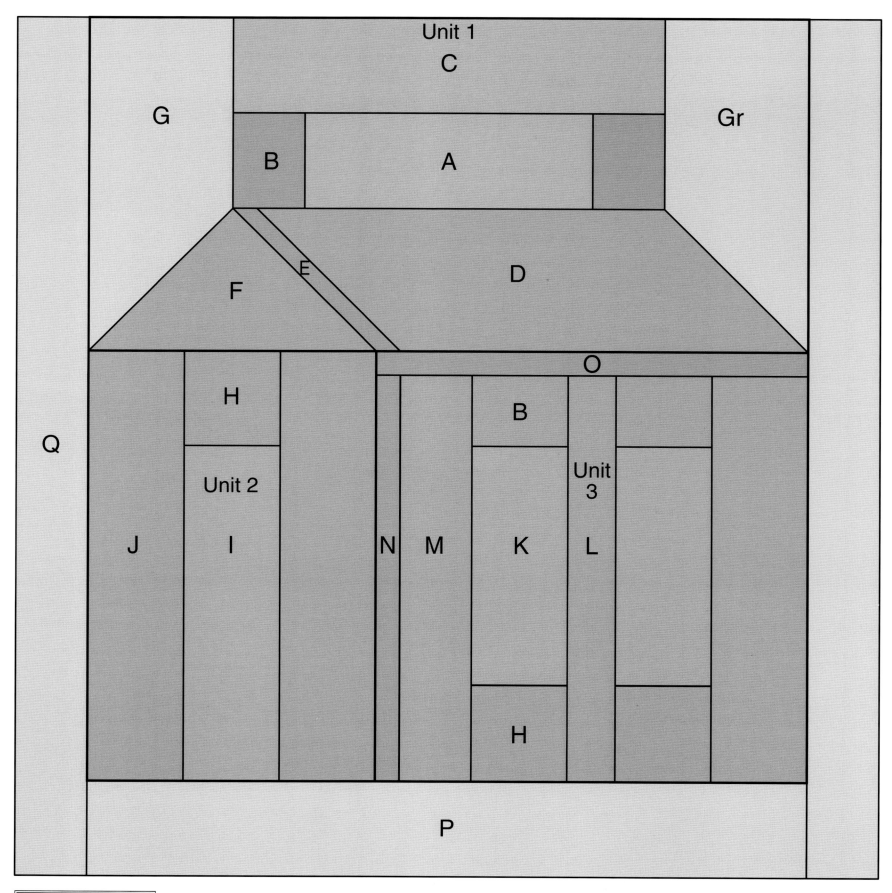

Unit 1

G

Gr

C

B

A

E

F

D

Q

O

H

Unit 2

J

I

N

M

B

Unit 3

K

L

H

P

These blocks are inspired by the antique quilt on page 104, top.

How to Construct This Block

Row 1: Sew M to the right side of A, B, and C. Add M to the left side of A. Sew Row 1 together, pressing seams in one direction. Alternate pressing direction with each subsequent row.

Row 2: Sew N to the right side of D, E, and F. Add N to the left side of D. Sew Row 2 together.

Row 3: Sew O to the right side of G, H, and I. Add O to the left side of G. Sew Row 3 together.

Row 4: Sew P to the right side of J, K, and L. Add P to the left side of J. Sew Row 4 together.

Lay out the rows, beginning and ending with Q, in nine horizontal rows. Stitch the rows together to complete the block. Press the seams in one direction.

How to Make This Quilt

This quilt is designed to be a twin-size quilt measuring 63×90 inches, including a 9-inch inner border and a 4½-inch pieced outer border.

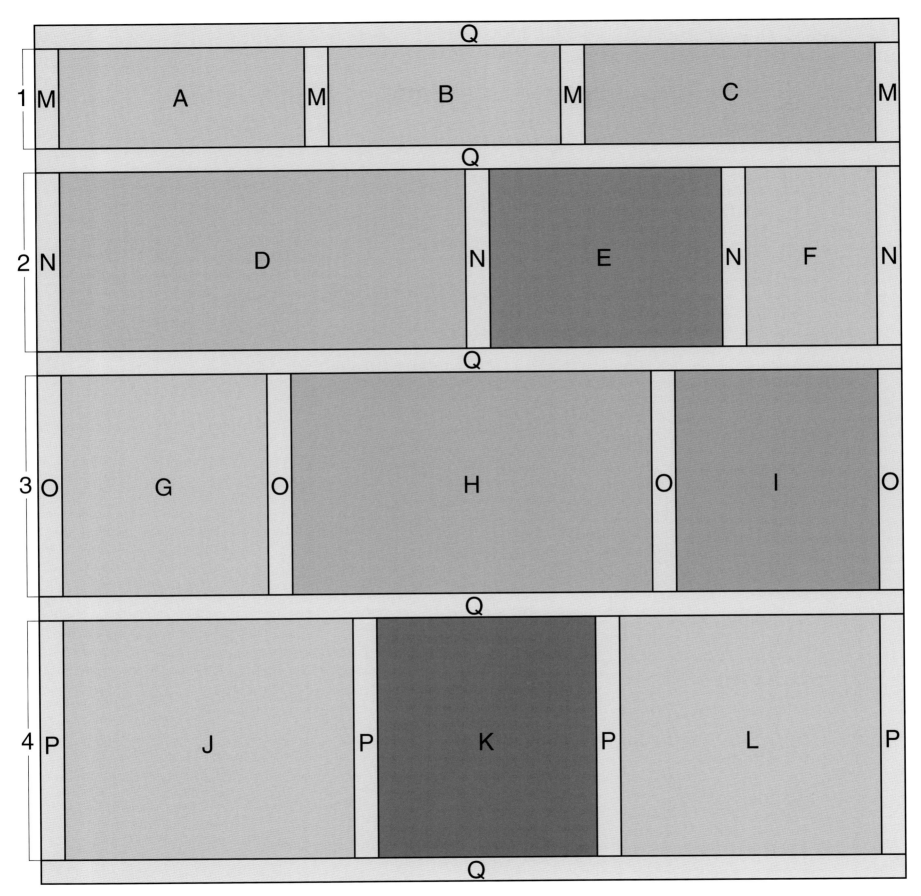

TILE BLOCK
full-size block

Tile Heart

These blocks are inspired by the antique quilt on page 104, top.

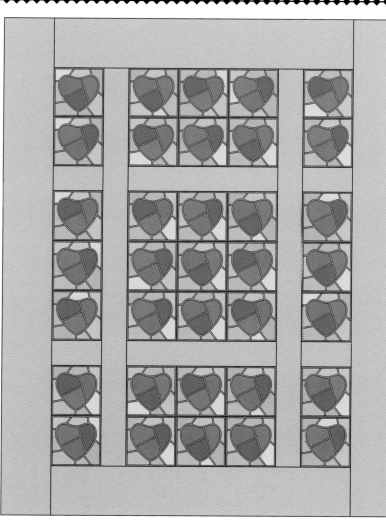

How to Construct This Block

Mark a ¼-inch seam allowance around the outside edge of a 9½-inch background square, using a quilter's pencil or water-soluble pen. Each appliqué piece is separated by a ¼-inch space, allowing the background to frame the appliquéd pieces. Spacing is critical to the look of this block, and basting the seam allowance under on each piece is recommended. After appliqué pieces have been basted, arrange pieces, beginning with A, on the background square. Carefully measure the ¼-inch seam allowance space. Pin or baste in place and appliqué pieces with matching threads. Remove the ¼-inch markings on the quilt block.

How to Make This Quilt

This quilt is designed to be a twin-size quilt measuring 72×90 inches, including 4½-inch sashing and a 9-inch border.

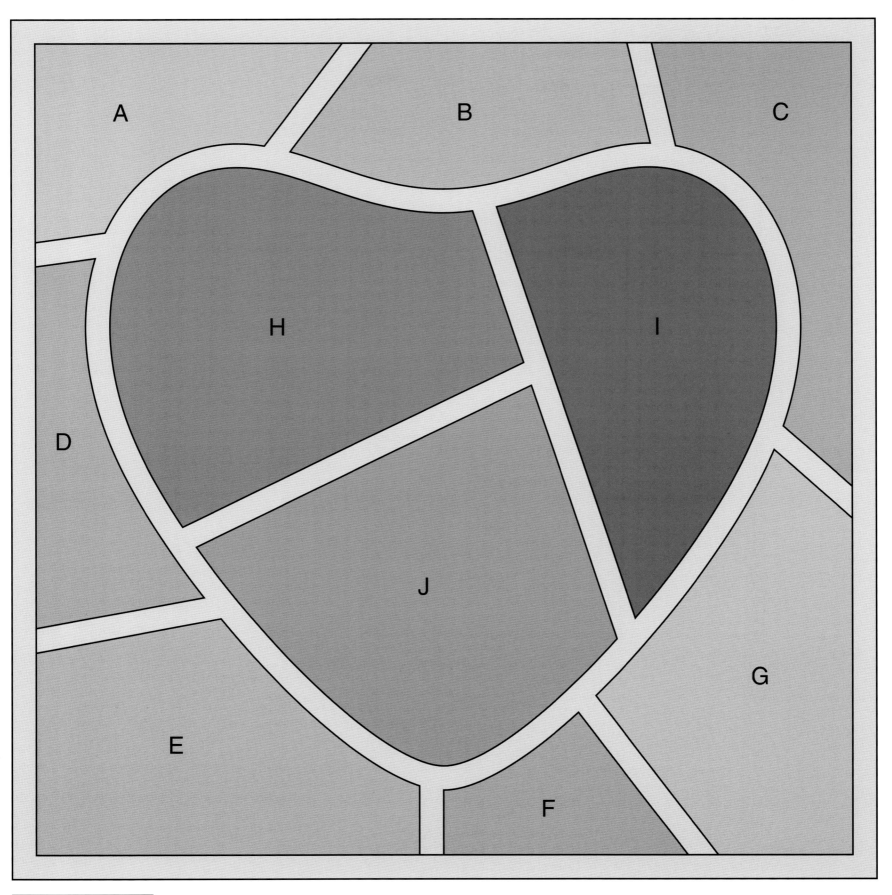

1890-1920 Sawtooth

These blocks are inspired by the antique quilt on page 103, top.

How to Construct This Block

Sew B to B to make the center square. Sew A to A (20 times). Sew four A squares together (2 times). Stitch one unit to the left side of the B square and one unit to the right side of the B square, noting color direction. Sew six A squares together (2 times). Stitch one unit to the top and one to the bottom of the AB unit.

How to Make This Quilt

This quilt is designed to be a twin-size quilt measuring 72×90 inches.

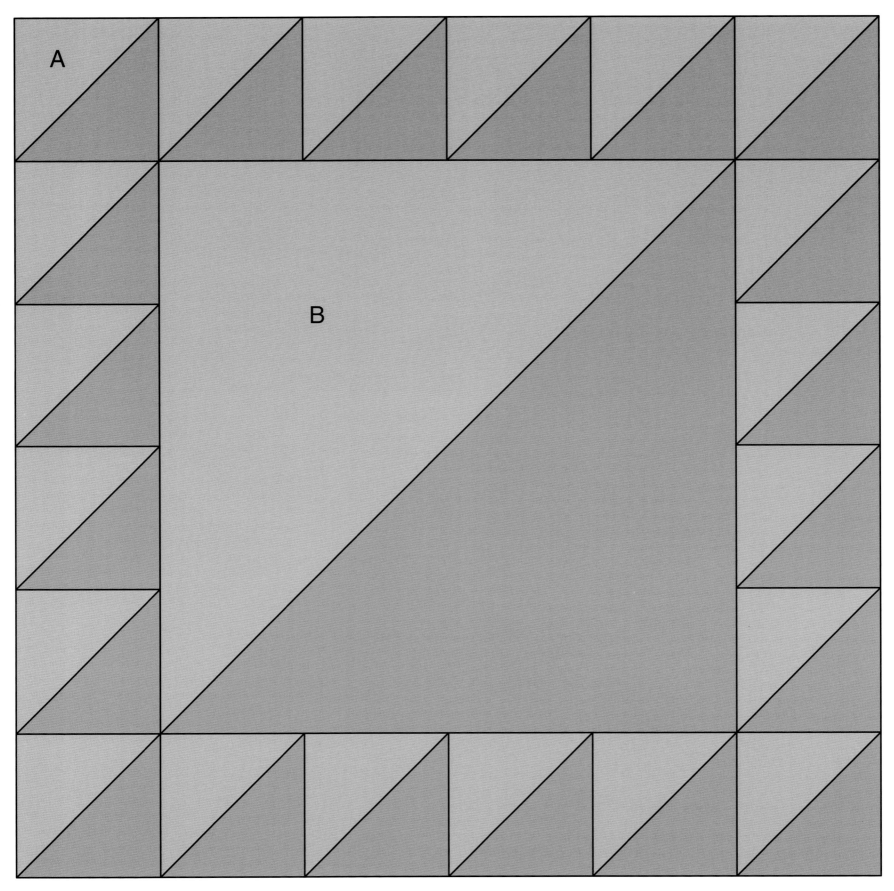

A

B

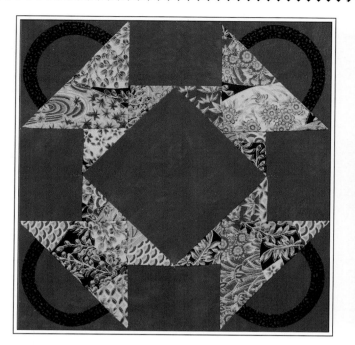

These blocks are inspired by the antique quilt on pages 102 and 103, bottom.

How to Construct This Block

Appliqué E to dark A, using matching thread (4 times). Sew dark A to light A (4 times). Sew B to C (4 times). Sew B to a reversed position of C (4 times). Sew BC to the right side of AA (4 times). Sew BC reversed to the left side of AABC (4 times) to complete a basket unit. Sew ABC to opposite sides of D. Set in ABC to the remaining two sides of D. Stop the stitching at the seam line of ABCD. Reposition ABC and begin stitching at the seam line. Be careful not to stitch through the ABCD seam line. Stop the stitching at the next ABCD, reposition the ABC, and begin stitching at the seam line.

How to Make This Quilt

This quilt is designed to be a twin-size quilt measuring 76½×94½ inches with 9-inch setting blocks. The inner border is 2¼ inches and the outer border is the Flying Geese border from *page 209.*

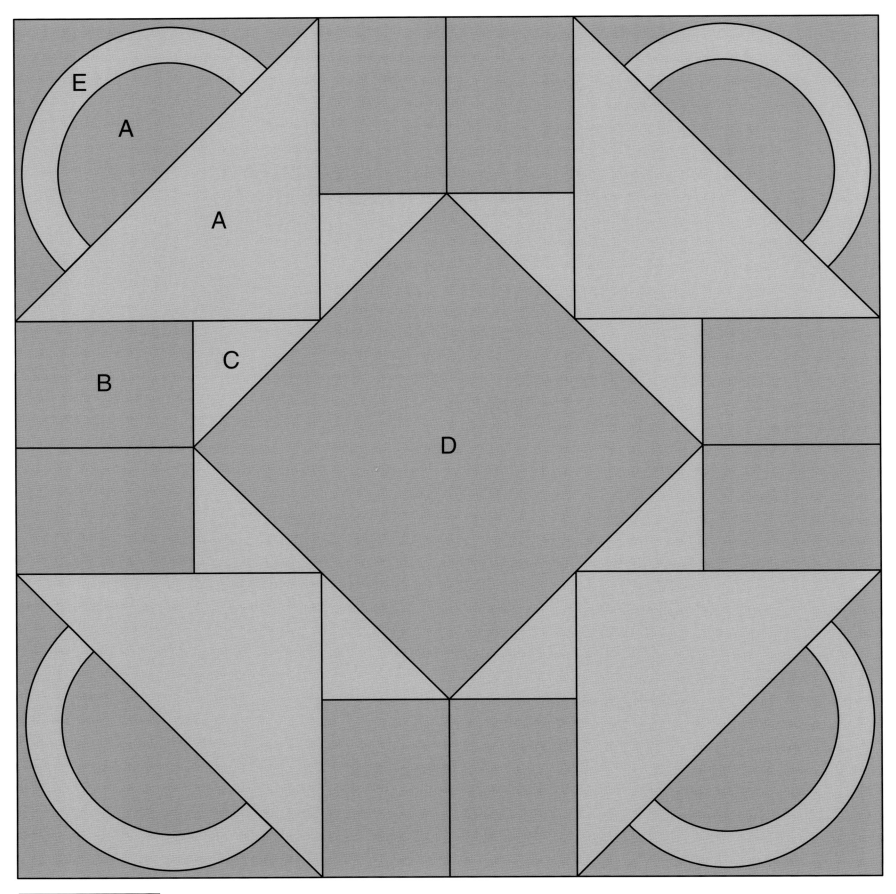

BASKET
full-size block

These blocks are inspired by the antique quilt on page 108, top.

How to Construct This Block

To make templates, mark where the points of A, Ar, B, and C meet using a hole punch. Mark the fabric through the hole, pinning the pieces together to match each point. Each time you sew a piece together, stop the stitching at the point, and knot or backstitch. Set in all of the pieces except D. Sew B to B (2 times). Sew BB to BB. Sew A to the left side of B (4 times). Sew Ar to the right side of B (4 times). Sew the right side of C to the left side of ABAr (4 times). Sew the left side of CABAr to the right side of CABAr (4 times). Appliqué D in the center of the block. If desired, embroider a signature in the center of the D square.

How to Make This Quilt

This quilt is designed to be a king-size quilt measuring 105×117¾ inches. The blocks are set on point and the Starry Scallop border from *page 212* without appliqué finishes the quilt.

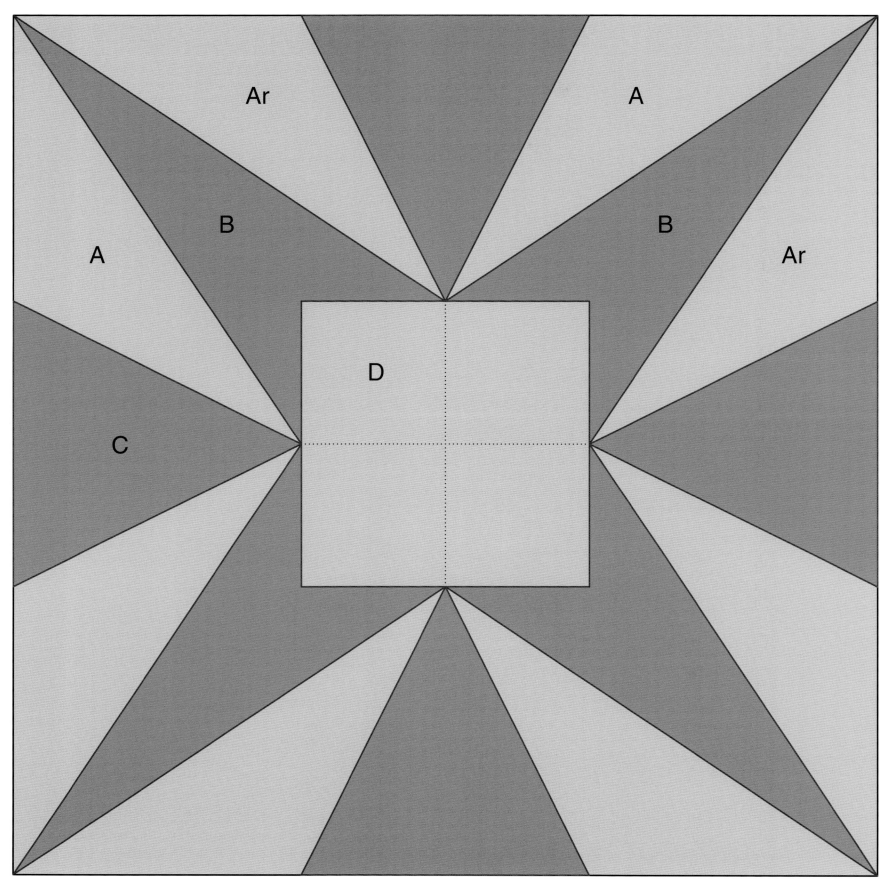

AUTOGRAPH STAR
full-size block

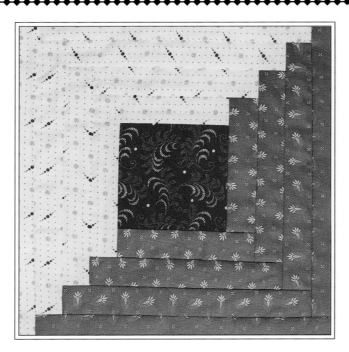

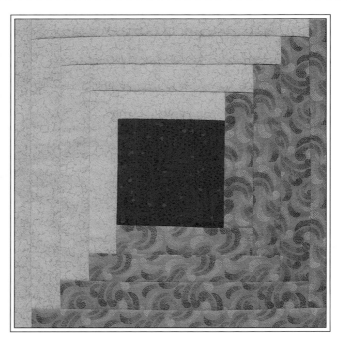

These blocks are inspired by the antique quilts on pages 65, top, and 107, bottom.

How to Construct This Block

In a clockwise direction, sew light B to A. Press seam allowance toward B. Add dark C to the right side of AB. Press seam allowance toward C. Add dark C to ABC. Continue sewing each strip in alphabetical order to the center unit, pressing toward the strip that has been added, ending with the J strip to complete the block.

Alternate method:
Cut an A square and assorted light and dark strips to 1½ inches wide. As each strip is sewn to the center unit, press seams toward the strip. Trim the edges even with the center unit. Continue clockwise adding strips until a 9½-inch block is completed, including seam allowances.

How to Make This Quilt

This quilt is designed to be a full-size quilt measuring 81×99 inches, including Stripes Around border from *page 206* as shown. When cutting the corners, add seam allowances.

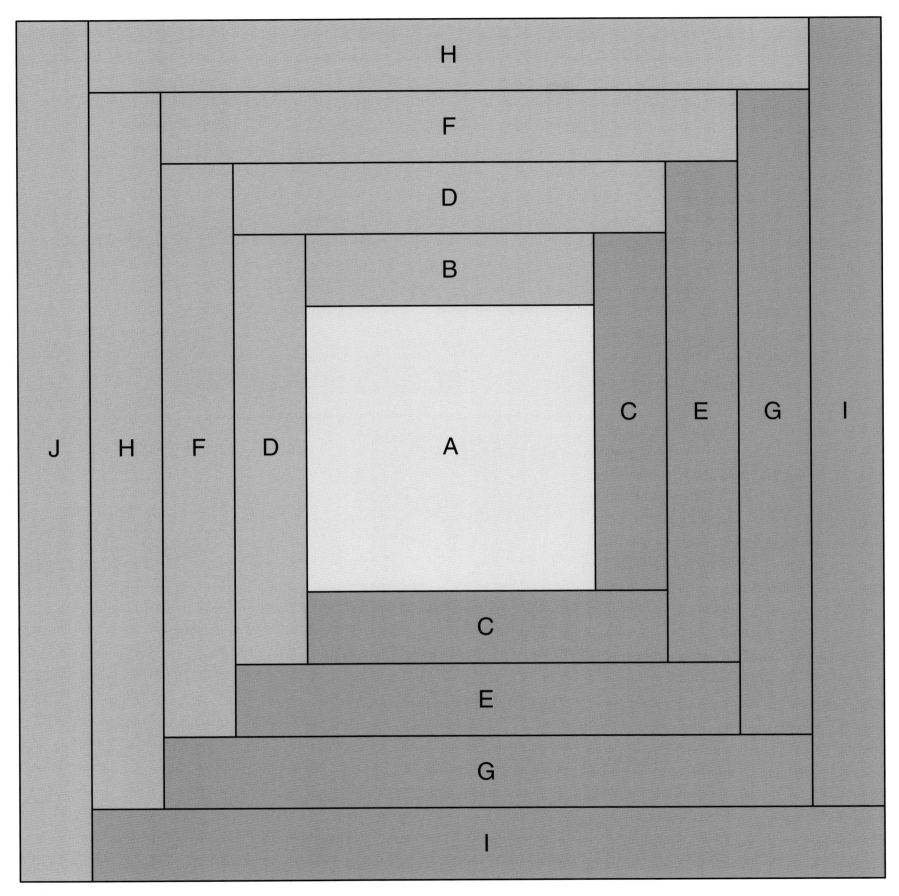

These blocks are inspired by the antique quilt on page 104, bottom.

How to Construct This Block

Sew A to opposite sides of B. Press seams toward A. To the remaining two sides of B, sew A. Press seams toward A. Trace the embroidery pattern onto the block. Using the diagrams on *page 199*, embroider the flower using two strands of embroidery thread or one strand of pearl cotton. The flower centers are French knots. The flower petals are straight stitches. The stem and leaves are stem stitches. The blocks are outlined as shown using featherstitches with straight-stitch accents in each corner.

How to Make This Quilt

This quilt is designed to be a twin-size quilt measuring 72×90 inches with embroidered blocks alternating with plain blocks. The Diamond Link border from *page 205* finishes the quilt.

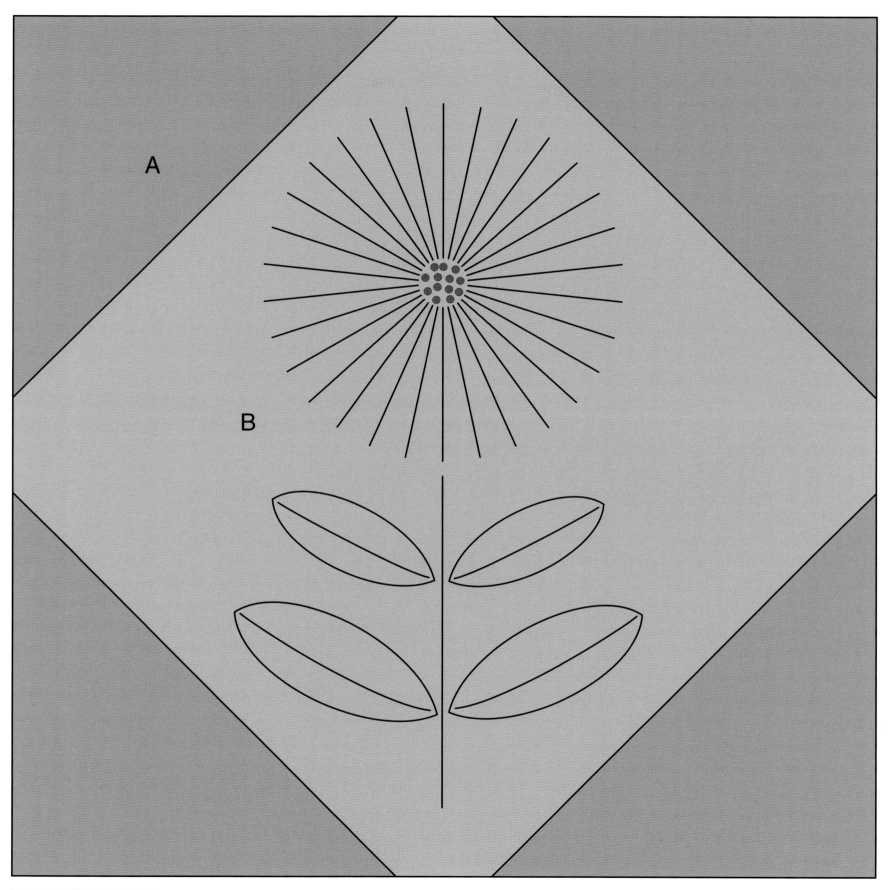

A

B

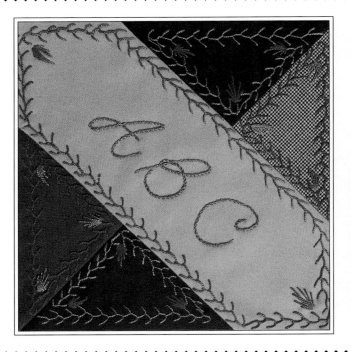

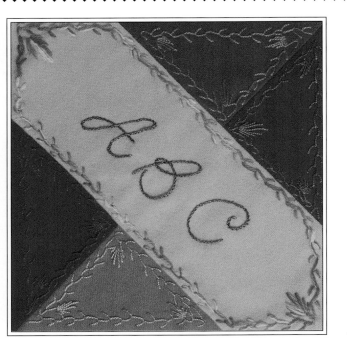

These blocks are inspired by the antique quilt on page 104, bottom.

How to Construct This Block

Sew medium A to dark A (2 times). To each long side of B, sew AA. Fold the block diagonally in half along the seam lines of AA to find the center placement for the middle initial. Enlarge the letter patterns from *page 213* to the desired size. Trace the letters onto the block. Embroider the block using two strands of embroidery thread or one strand of pearl cotton. Complete the monogram using stem stitches (see stitch diagrams on *page 199*). The pieces are outlined as shown using featherstitches with straight-stitch accents.

How to Make This Quilt

This quilt is designed to be a full-size quilt measuring 81×99 inches. The blocks are rotated to create the lattice effect. The outer Diamond border is from *page 203* and uses 4½-inch plain corner squares.

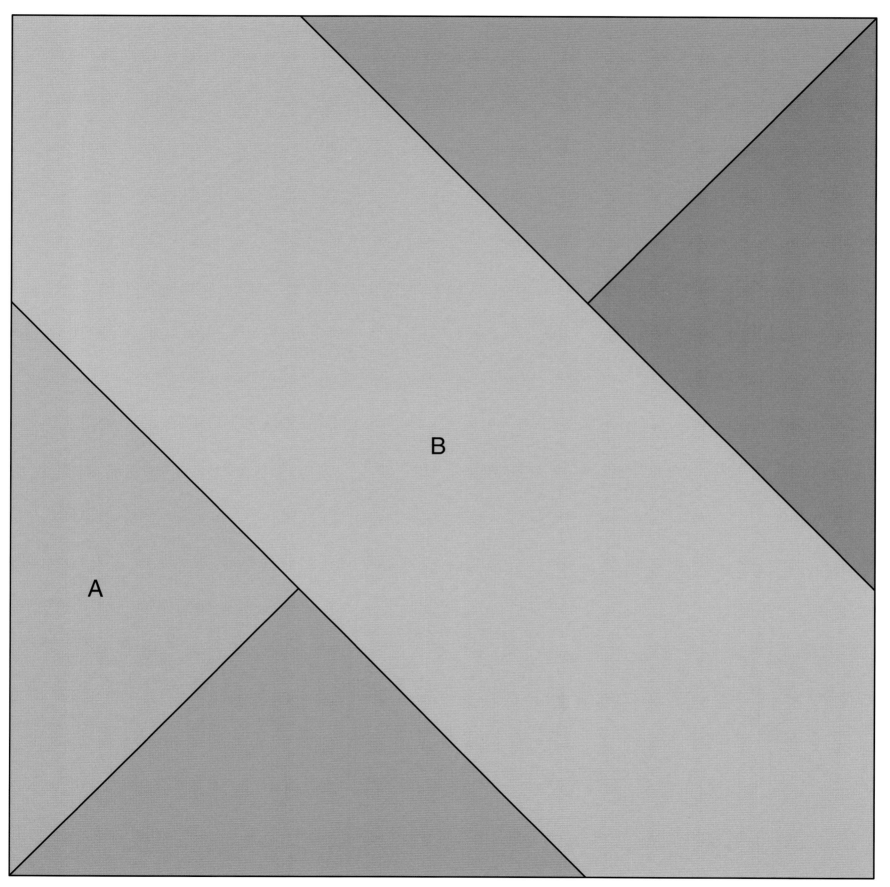

A

B

These blocks are inspired by the antique quilt on page 108, bottom.

How to Construct This Block

Repeat the following directions four times to complete five Nine-Patch blocks. Sew dark A to light A (3 times). To AA, sew a dark A (2 times) for the top and bottom rows. To AA, sew a light A for middle row. Join the three rows to complete one Nine-Patch. Sew a Nine-Patch block to opposite sides of B (2 times) for Rows 1 and 3. Sew B to opposite sides of a Nine-Patch block for Row 2. Join the rows to complete one block.

How to Make This Quilt

This quilt is designed to be a twin-size quilt measuring 72×90 inches.

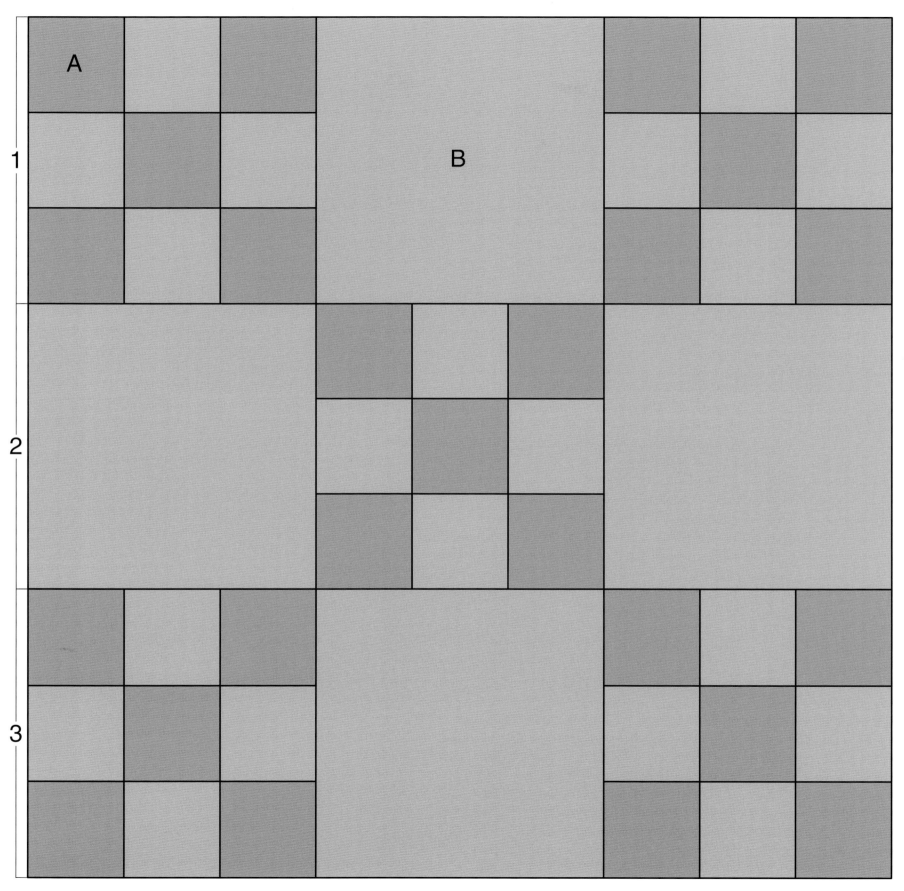

IRISH CHAIN
full-size block

These blocks are inspired by the antique quilt on page 111.

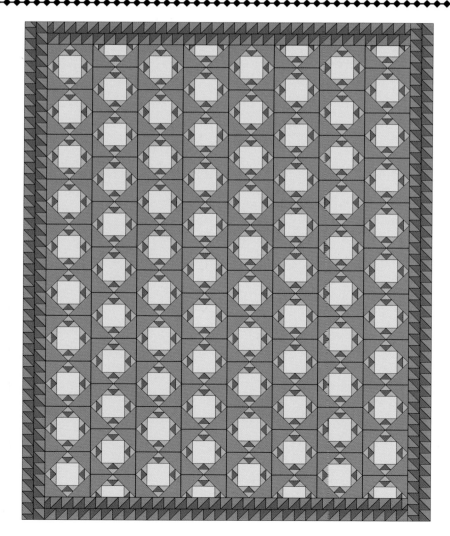

How to Construct This Block

Sew light A to medium A to make a triangle-square (4 times). Sew a light A to adjacent sides of AA (4 times). Sew AAA to opposite sides of B. Sew AAA to the remaining two sides of B. Sew C to opposite sides of the center unit. Sew C to the remaining two sides of the center unit.

How to Make This Quilt

This quilt is designed to be a full-size quilt measuring 81×99 inches with half-blocks at the top and bottom. The outer Zigzag border is from *page 204*.

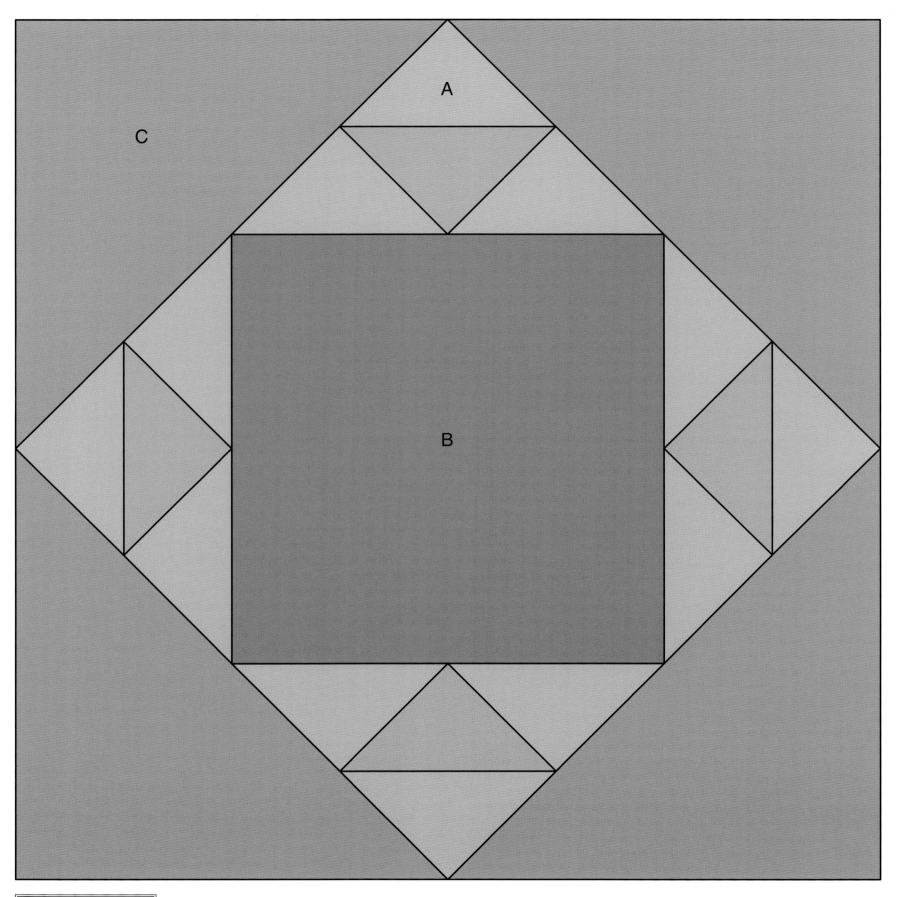

ROAD TO PARIS
full-size block

Windowpane

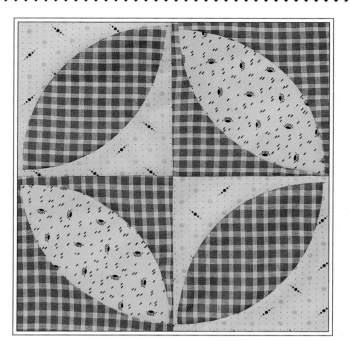

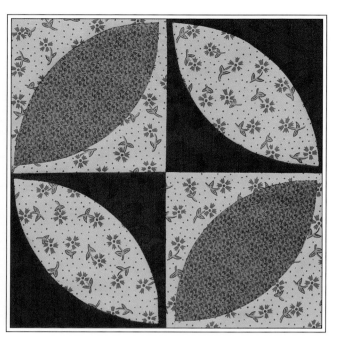

These blocks are inspired by the antique quilt on page 108, top.

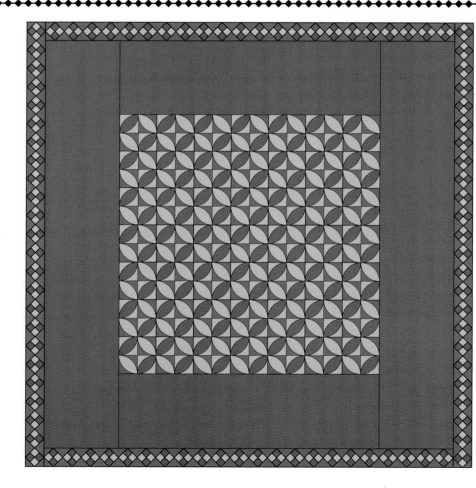

How to Construct This Block

This block may be pieced or appliquéd.

To piece:
Transfer the pattern placement marks to the templates. Mark each fabric piece with the placement marks. Pin two pieces together, matching marks and easing the pieces together while sewing. Sew A to B (4 times); add C (4 times). Sew ABC to ABC (2 times). Sew ABCABC to ABCABC.

To appliqué:
Appliqué B to a 5-inch A background square (4 times), using matching thread. Sew AB to AB (2 times). Sew ABAB to ABAB.

How to Make This Quilt

This quilt is designed to be a queen-size quilt measuring 99×99 inches, including a 13½-inch plain inner border and the outer Diamond Link border from *page 205*.

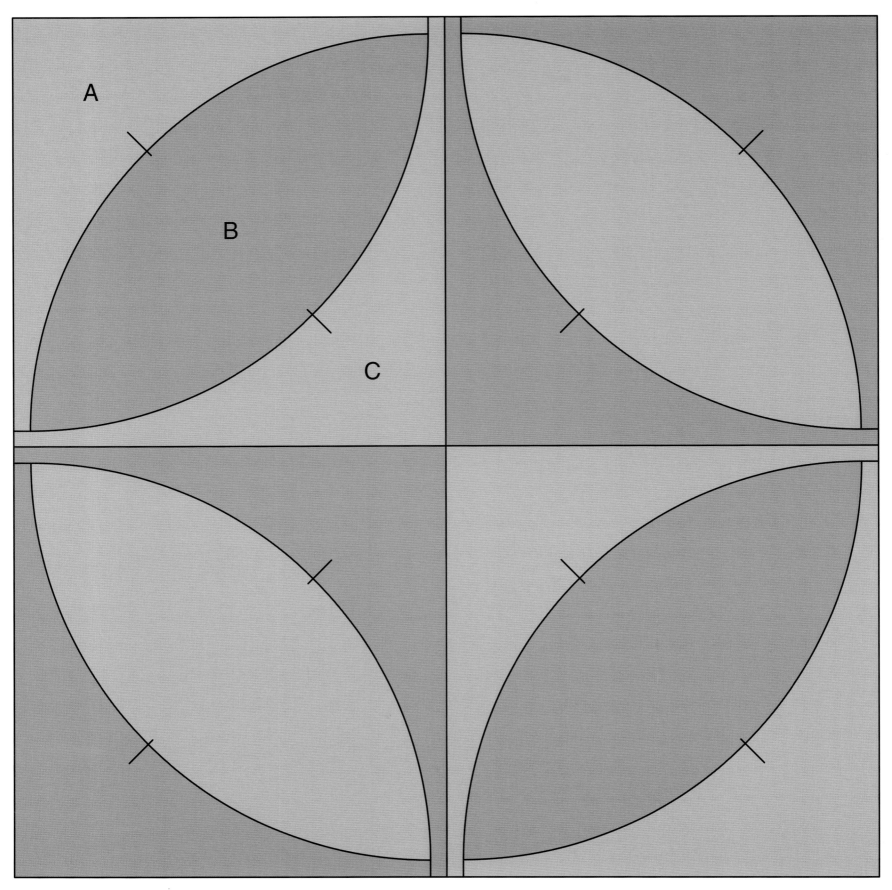

A

B

C

How to Construct This Block

Sew a light A to a medium A (8 times). Sew a light A to a medium-light A (4 times). Sew a light A to a dark A (4 times). Following the pattern for placement, lay out the triangle-squares. Sew AA to AA (8 times). Join AAAA to AAAA (4 times). Stitch Row 1 and Row 2 together. Stitch Row 3 and Row 4. Join the two units to complete the block.

How to Make This Quilt

This quilt is designed to be a full- or queen-size quilt measuring 90×99 inches, including a 4½-inch inner border, two 2¼-inch middle borders, and a 9-inch outer border with quilt block corners.

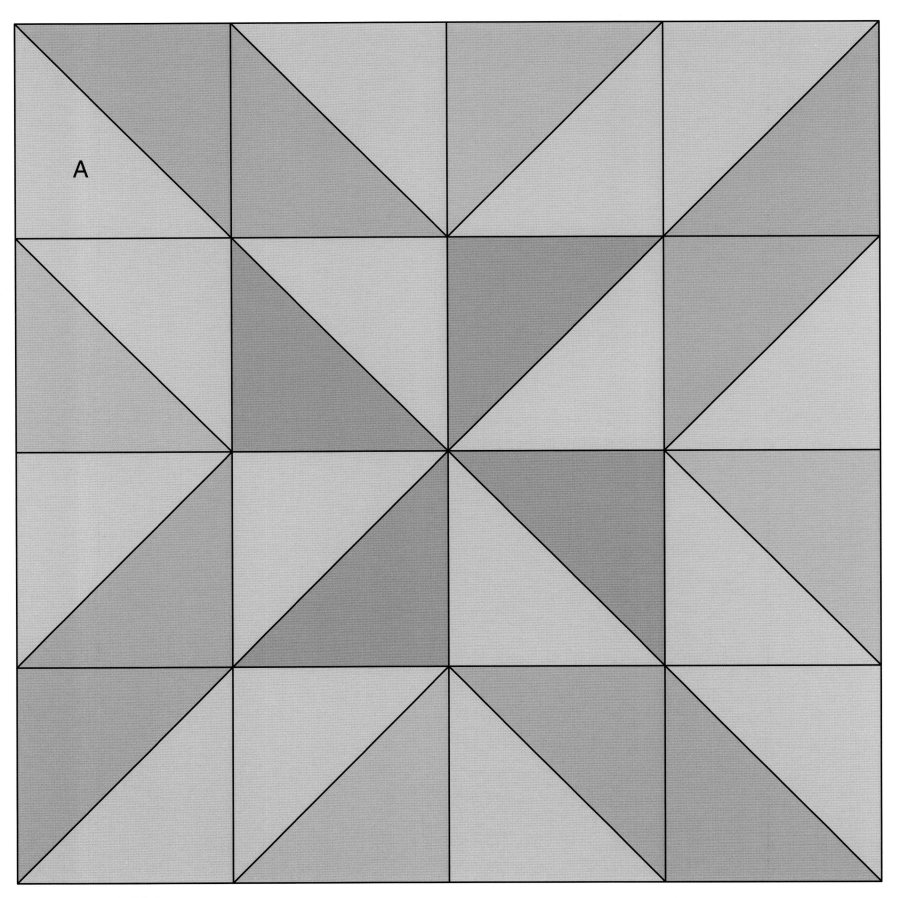

A

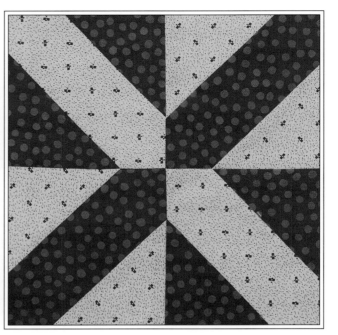

These blocks are inspired by the antique quilt on page 105.

How to Construct This Block

Sew a dark A to a light B; add a dark A (2 times). Sew a light A to a dark B; add a light A (2 times). Sew a dark ABA to a light ABA (2 times). Stitch the two units together, reversing positions of the light and dark units.

How to Make This Quilt

This quilt is designed to be a twin-size quilt measuring 72×90 inches, including the Diamond border from *page 203* with corner blocks.

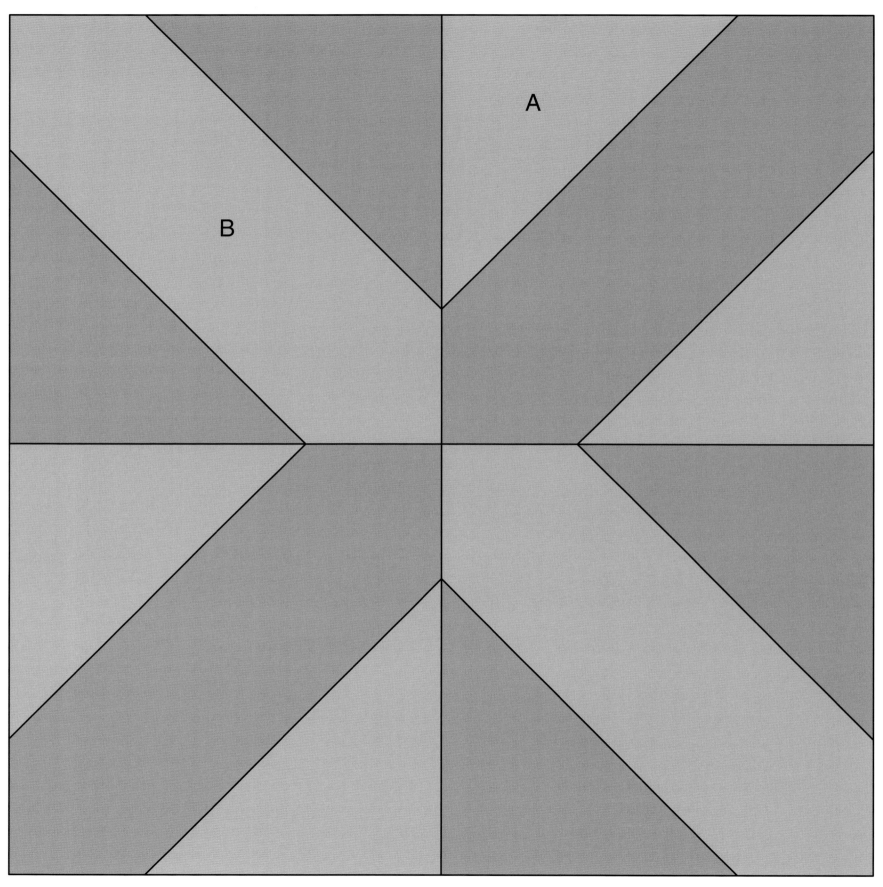

A

B

LATTICE
full-size block

These blocks are inspired by the antique quilt on page 106.

How to Construct This Block

Sew light A to dark Ar (4 times). Sew dark A to light Ar (4 times). Sew light AAr to dark AAr (4 times); add B (4 times). Set in C to AArB unit (8 times). Stop the stitching at the seam line of AAr. Reposition C and begin stitching at the seam line. Set in D to AArBC (4 times). Stop the stitching at ArA. Reposition D and begin stitching at the seam line. Sew E to the right side of AArBCD (2 times). Sew the left side of AArBCD to AArBCDE (2 times) to make Rows 1 and 3. Sew a short side of E to F; add E to make Row 2. Stitch Row 1 to Row 2; add Row 3.

How to Make This Quilt

This quilt is designed to be a queen-size quilt measuring 94½×107¼ inches. The quilt center blocks are set on point with 4½-inch sashing and setting squares. The outer triangles are one-half of the block on point. These triangles need to have the seam allowance added. The outer border is 9 inches with corner blocks.

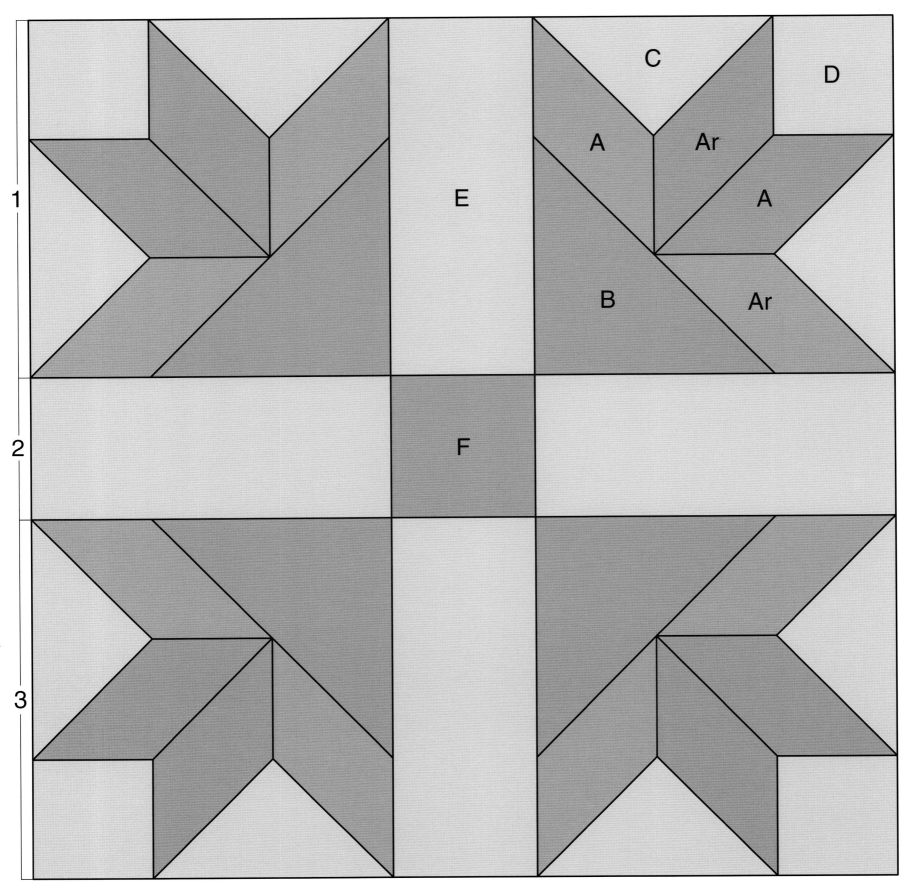

GOOSE TRACKS
full-size block

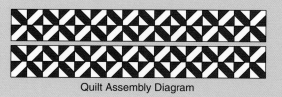

Quilt Assembly Diagram

Lattice Quilt

Pictured on page 105.

This antique quilt uses the backing fabric as binding by folding and rolling the back over the quilt top seam allowance and hand-stitching it in place. Separate yardage has been given for binding if you choose not to roll the backing to the top.

Materials

3⅝ yards of red fabric
3⅝ yards of white fabric

4⅞ yards of backing fabric
⅝ yards of binding fabric (optional)
78×87-inch piece of quilt batting

Finished quilt: 72×81 inches
Finished quilt block: 9 inches square
    Quantities specified are for 44/45-inch-wide 100 percent cotton fabrics. Measurements include a ¼-inch seam allowance.

Cut the Fabric

To make the best use of fabrics, cut the pieces in the following order.
From red fabric, cut:
288 of Pattern A;
144 of Pattern B
From white fabric, cut:
288 of Pattern A,
144 of Pattern B
From binding fabric, cut:
8—2½×42-inch strips (optional)

Make the Blocks

Complete 72 red-and-white blocks, following the directions on *page 138* and noting color placement.

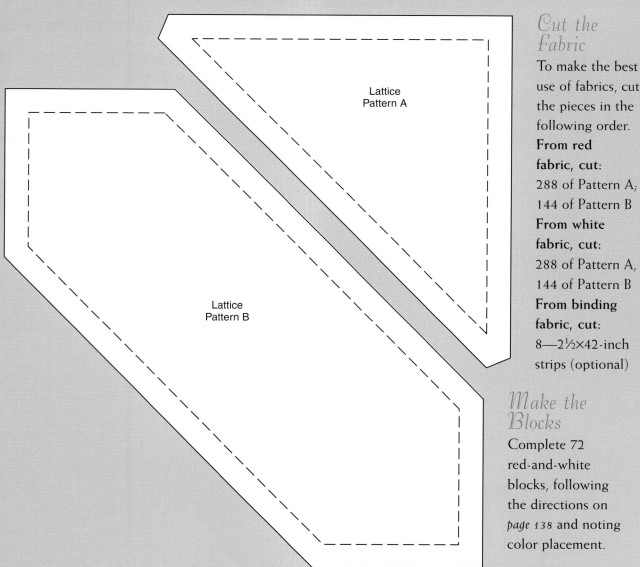

Lattice
Pattern A

Lattice
Pattern B

Assemble the Quilt Center

1. Referring to the Quilt Assembly Diagram for placement, lay out the Lattice blocks in nine horizontal rows containing eight blocks each. Sew the blocks together in each row. Press the seam allowances in one direction, alternating the direction with each row.

2. Join the rows to make the quilt center. Press the seam allowances in one direction. The pieced quilt top should measure 72½×81½, including the seam allowances.

Complete the Quilt

1. Layer the quilt top, batting, and backing.
2. Quilt as desired. Bind as desired.

Goose Tracks Quilt

Pictured on page 106.

Materials

4½ yards of pink print for blocks, setting blocks, and borders
2½ yards of cream print for block background and binding
1½ yards of black print for blocks
5 yards of backing fabric
76×90-inch piece of quilt batting

Finished quilt: 70×84¼ inches
Finished block: 10 inches square
    Quantities specified are for 44/45-inch-wide, 100 percent cotton fabrics. All measurements include a ¼-inch seam allowance unless otherwise specified.

Cut the Fabric

To make the best use of fabrics, cut the pieces in the following order. The border

Quilt Assembly Diagram

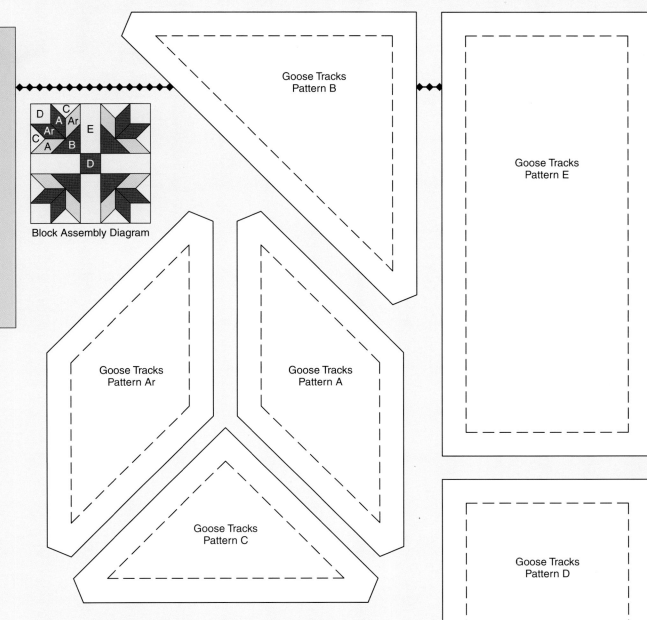

Block Assembly Diagram

Goose Tracks Pattern B

Goose Tracks Pattern E

Goose Tracks Pattern Ar

Goose Tracks Pattern A

Goose Tracks Pattern C

Goose Tracks Pattern D

strips are cut parallel to the selvage of the fabric. The listings include the mathematically correct border lengths. You may wish to add extra length to the borders to allow for any sewing differences. Trim the border strips to the actual length before adding them to the quilt top.

The following directions include cutting instructions to complete 20 unfinished Goose Tracks blocks. For piecing directions, see *page 140*.

From pink print, cut:
2—7×84¾-inch border strips
2—7×57½-inch border strips
4—15½-inch squares, cutting each
    diagonally twice in an X for a total of 16
    setting triangles (you will only use 14)
2—8-inch squares, cutting each in half
    diagonally for a total of 4 corner triangles
12—10½-inch squares for setting squares
80 each of Patterns A and Ar

From cream print, cut:
8—2½×42-inch binding strips
80 of Pattern E; 160 of Pattern C
80 of Pattern D

From black print, cut:
80 each of Patterns A and Ar
80 of Pattern B; 20 of Pattern D

Make the Blocks
Complete 20 blocks, following the directions on *page 140*.

Assemble the Quilt Center
1. Referring to the Quilt Assembly Diagram, *above*, lay out the 20—10½-inch Goose Tracks blocks, 12—10½-inch pink print setting squares, and 14 pink print setting triangles in diagonal rows. The corner triangles are added later.
2. Sew together blocks in each diagonal row. Press seam allowances toward pink print setting squares and triangles. Join rows. Add four pink print corner triangles to make quilt center. Press

seams in one direction. The quilt center should measure 57½×71¾ inches including seam allowances.

Add the Borders
1. Sew one 7×57½-inch pink print border to top and bottom of quilt center.
2. Sew a 7×84¾-inch pink print border to each side of the quilt center.

Complete the Quilt
1. Layer the quilt top, batting, and backing.
2. Quilt as desired. Bind the quilt using the cream print binding strips.

143

1920-1950

Reflecting the prosperity of the 1920s and the Great Depression of the 1930s and beyond, quilts from this era showed quilters' love for the beauty of quilting. In the 1920s quilting patterns were published and quilting columns appeared in printed publications, supporting the timeless art form. Colors were lovely and lively, enjoying the best of times and defying the worst of times. Only a World War could dampen quilters' needs to create.

Period Quilt History

The 1920s were years of prosperity and change. By 1921 women had won the right to vote and were liberated from household drudgeries of the past. Electricity, gas, water lines, automobiles, telephones, and new washing and sewing machines revolutionized American life.

Encouraged by new products and vast published materials, American women experienced renewed interest in making quilts. The nationwide publication of quilt patterns during the 1920s and 1930s altered the quilting tradition. Many newspapers and national magazines printed quilting columns during the 1920s. For the first time, quilters in all parts of the country saw the same patterns and fabric suggestions at the same time.

The crash of Wall Street in 1929 and the Great

CORNUCOPIAS
c.1933

FOUR FLOWER- AND LEAF-LADEN CORNUCOPIAS EMBELLISH THE CORNERS OF THIS FINE COTTON QUILT WITH MORE LEAVES AND FLOWERS SET IN THE QUILT CENTER. THE QUILT DISPLAYS FINE APPLIQUÉ AND BUTTONHOLE STITCHES AROUND EACH PIECE. FULL INSTRUCTIONS ARE NOT AVAILABLE FOR THIS QUILT. FOR THE BLOCK INSPIRED BY THIS QUILT, SEE PAGE 174.
Courtesy: University of Nebraska-Lincoln

APPLIQUÉD POPPIES
c.1925

LONG-STEMMED YELLOW AND GOLD FLOWERS TAKE CENTER STAGE IN THIS APPLIQUÉD COTTON QUILT. FULL INSTRUCTIONS ARE NOT AVAILABLE FOR THIS QUILT. FOR THE BLOCK INSPIRED BY THIS QUILT, SEE PAGE 166.
Courtesy: University of Nebraska-Lincoln

GRANDMOTHER'S FAN
c.1930

THIS BEAUTIFUL EXAMPLE OF GRANDMOTHER'S FAN WAS SKILLFULLY MACHINE-PIECED IN THE MIDWEST. THE FAN BLADES ARE MADE OF MUSLIN AND SHIRTING FABRICS. FULL INSTRUCTIONS ARE NOT AVAILABLE FOR THIS QUILT. FOR THE BLOCK INSPIRED BY THIS QUILT, SEE PAGE 156. *Courtesy: University of Nebraska-Lincoln*

Depression of the 1930s brought hard times to America.

Many quilts made during this time contradict the difficult times. Regardless of pattern or plan of origin, most 1930s quilts were pretty, pastel, and surprisingly sophisticated.

Although quilting was a magazine tradition dating back to *Godey's Lady's Book* of the 1800s, it was new for newspapers and very successful. A 1930 Gallup survey named quilt columns as the most popular feature in six major city newspapers.

Contests with prize money were offered at fairs for winning quilts. Because materials for prizewinning quilts were too expensive for many people, some used printed feed and grain sacks as well as their clothing and underwear to make quilts. Considered charming today, the use of sacks labeled the maker as poor or frugal and from a rural community.

BABY BUNTING FANS
c.1935

A QUILTER IN CASS COUNTY, ILLINOIS, MADE THIS BABY BUNTING FANS QUILT. THE QUILT IS WORKED IN NINE 22-INCH BLOCKS WITH PURPLE SASHING AND A SCALLOP BORDER. FULL INSTRUCTIONS ARE NOT AVAILABLE FOR THIS QUILT. FOR THE BLOCK INSPIRED BY THIS QUILT, SEE PAGE 172.
Courtesy: University of Nebraska-Lincoln

POSTAGE STAMP, TRIP AROUND THE WORLD
c.1930

THIS HAND-PIECED WORK OF ART IS A WONDERFUL EXAMPLE OF THE POSTAGE STAMP OR TRIP AROUND THE WORLD. THE ¾-INCH COTTON SQUARES APPEAR AS ORGANIZED POSTAGE STAMPS. EACH BLOCK IS CONTAINED BY A ROW OF BLACK AND A ROW OF SMALL RED AND WHITE CHECKS. THE TRIPLE PINK, GREEN, AND BLACK BORDERS EACH HAVE A ROW OF CABLE QUILTING. FULL INSTRUCTIONS ARE NOT AVAILABLE FOR THIS QUILT. FOR THE BLOCK INSPIRED BY THIS QUILT, SEE PAGE 160. *Courtesy: University of Nebraska-Lincoln*

A PIECE OF QUILTING HISTORY

Throughout time, quilting parties have been tightly woven into the social fabric. While visiting just for fun was not tolerated in early times, it was permissible for groups of women from farms miles apart to gather and busy themselves (and gossip) at a quilting frame.

Getting by during the Great Depression meant relearning the skills of earlier days. With the changing times, quiltmaking incorporated the old and the new. Although Depression-era quilts were based on traditional patterns and techniques, strong colors of authentic early patchwork clashed with the styles of the 1930s. Pastel colors and the influence of such design styles as Art Deco and Art Nouveau incorporated with old designs to create a new look. By concentrating on making beautiful quilts, quilters could block out poverty and deprivation.

When the United States entered into World War II in 1941, the quilting revival declined. During the war, women went to

DECO SHOOTING STAR
c. 1925

A COMBINATION OF MACHINE AND HAND PIECING, THE DARK BLUE AND ORANGE COTTON FABRICS CREATE A BOLD DESIGN ON A WHITE BACKGROUND. THE PIECED BLOCKS HAVE AN EIGHT-POINTED STAR AT THE TOP WITH A PENDANT SHAPE POINTING DOWN. THE FINE HAND QUILTING IS QUAKER FEATHER AND OUTLINE PATTERNS. FULL INSTRUCTIONS ARE NOT AVAILABLE FOR THIS QUILT. FOR THE BLOCK INSPIRED BY THIS QUILT, SEE PAGE 154.
Courtesy: University of Nebraska-Lincoln

A PIECE OF QUILTING HISTORY

"You can spoil the prettiest quilt pieces that ever was made just by putting them together with the wrong color, just as the best sort of life is miserable if you don't look at things right and think about them right."

—ELIZA CALVERT HALL,
AUNT JANE OF KENTUCKY

MARTHA'S VINEYARD
c. 1925

AN ATTRACTIVE EXAMPLE OF THE KIT QUILTS POPULAR DURING THE PERIOD, THIS COTTON VERSION OF MARTHA'S VINEYARD WAS MADE IN OHIO. THE CENTER IS MADE UP OF SIX BUNCHES OF STUFFED GRAPES. FULL INSTRUCTIONS ARE NOT AVAILABLE FOR THIS QUILT. FOR THE BLOCK INSPIRED BY THIS QUILT, SEE PAGE 158.
Courtesy: University of Nebraska-Lincoln

SUNBONNET SUE
c.1930

THIS SUNBONNET SUE QUILT IS APPLIQUÉD OF MULTICOLOR COTTON SOLIDS AND PRINTS ON WHITE. THE DETAILS ARE EMBROIDERY, RIBBON, AND LACE TRIM. THE GIRLS AND BOYS ARE SET IN CONVERSATIONAL PAIRS, ACCOMPANIED BY MARCHING GEESE, CROSSES, A BEACH BALL, AND TREES, SURROUNDED BY A WHITE PICKET FENCE. FULL INSTRUCTIONS ARE NOT AVAILABLE FOR THIS QUILT. FOR THE BLOCKS INSPIRED BY THIS QUILT, SEE PAGES 168–171. *Courtesy: University of Nebraska-Lincoln*

SIGNATURE QUILT
c.1927

THE CENTER OF THIS SIGNATURE QUILT READS, "GOD BLESS THE M.E. HOME, ST. PAUL'S M.E. CHURCH, NEW YORK," AND "1927." THESE HAND-SCRIPTED LINES SUGGEST THAT THE QUILT WAS A FUND-RAISING PROJECT FOR THE CHURCH. MANY SIGNATURES, INCLUDING HARRY JAMES, ENRICO CARUSO WHO SANG IN THE BUFFALO AREA, AND SEVERAL CLERGY TITLES, ARE STITCHED IN BLUE FLOSS, PROBABLY AT A COST OF $1 EACH. INSTRUCTIONS ARE NOT AVAILABLE FOR THIS QUILT. FOR THE BLOCK INSPIRED BY THIS QUILT, SEE PAGE 192. *Courtesy: University of Nebraska-Lincoln*

work. After the war was over they transferred their attention to babies, mortgages, cars, and television—anything new and modern, rather than antique and colonial. Quiltmaking never died out, but it would be nearly 30 years before making quilts again became fashionable.

A PIECE OF QUILTING HISTORY

In the early days, quiltmakers exchanged patterns much as they exchanged recipes. Within the stitches of a Friendship Quilt you will see and feel the special love and bond that is shared by a group of women who quilt together. The Friendship Quilt, more than any other, preserves the tradition of fellowship that women have shared over the quilting frame for centuries. The memories and ties sewn into these quilts far exceed their value as bedcovers.

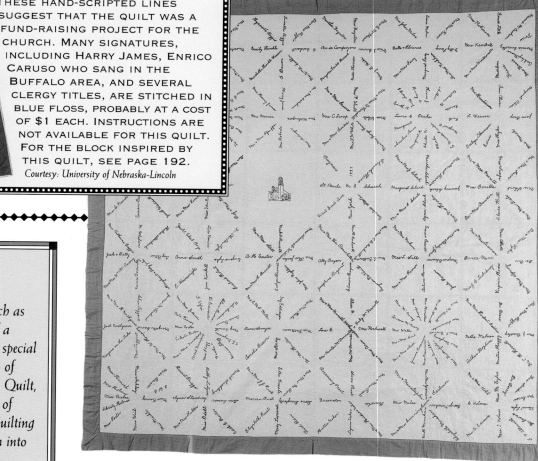

SIGNATURE QUILT BLOCKS
1920–1950
THESE BLOCKS WITH SIGNATURES
AND BIRTH DATES FROM WOMEN OF
ALL AGES WERE PURCHASED AT
AUCTION. DATES RANGE FROM
1931 TO 1937. *Courtesy: Margaret Sindelar*

PERIOD FABRICS
1920—1950

A SATIN-LINED SEWING BASKET
HOLDS PLAYFUL PRINTS—MANY
PRINTED ON FEED SACK FABRICS.

Courtesy: Margaret Sindelar

Fabrics Through Time

The influence of Art Deco is obvious in fabrics of the 1920s. Black and white squares and circles are distinctive of this period. Unlike the earlier period, the backgrounds for these prints were primarily white.

During the early 1900s, red with a slightly bluish overtone was introduced and often was used in combination with white for embroidered blocks that featured flowers, children, or animals. This fabric was often the "dark spot" on an otherwise pastel quilt.

Pinks regained popularity, especially a dusty rose. Favorite pink prints included gingham checks and reproduction calicos.

In juvenile prints, soft sky blue was indicative of the time.

As fabric dyes improved, reliable, colorfast hues were introduced, including mint green and bright purple. In the late 1920s a true orange appeared on the fabric scene and was used as a background color as well as an accent.

Although fabrics remained thin at the turn of the century, the quality improved during the 1920s. Original fabrics from this time often had a finishing glaze that provided sheen to the surface.

The most recognizable fabrics from the 1930s are printed, heavy-threaded feed sacks.

The prints of the time gave quilters huge options. There were dots, wavy lines, leaves, flowers, juvenile and novelty prints, and other playful motifs.

FOOL'S PUZZLE
c.1925

MADE FROM PRINTS AND SOLID COTTONS, THIS OHIO QUILT IS HAND- AND MACHINE-PIECED. A SINGLE ROW OF BLUE FANS CREATES THE SCALLOPED BORDER. INSTRUCTIONS ARE NOT AVAILABLE FOR THIS QUILT. FOR THE BLOCK INSPIRED BY THIS QUILT, SEE PAGE 164. *Courtesy: University of Nebraska-Lincoln*

REDS WITH MULTICOLORED PATTERNS WERE PRINTED ON WOVEN FABRIC.

PINKS, ESPECIALLY DUSTY ROSE, WERE POPULAR DURING THIS TIME.

PRINTS FROM THE 1920S OFTEN FEATURED CROSS-HATCHING BETWEEN PRINT MOTIFS.

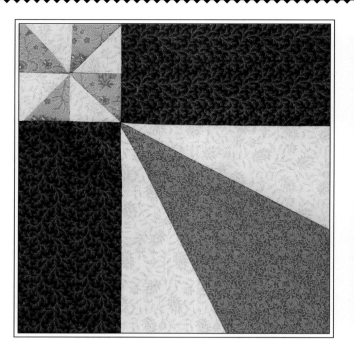

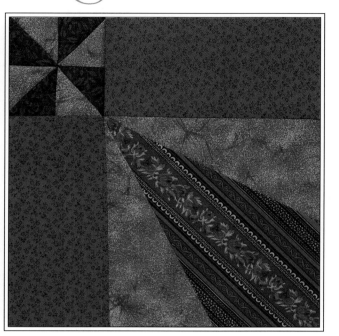

These blocks are inspired by the antique quilt on page 149, top.

HOW TO CONSTRUCT THIS BLOCK

Sew A to A (4 times). Sew AA to AA (2 times). Sew AAAA to AAAA to make Unit A. Sew B to C; add Br. Sew D to the left side of BrCB. Sew D to the right side of Unit A. Sew AD to BrCBD.

HOW TO MAKE THIS QUILT

This quilt is designed to be a king-size quilt measuring 101×101 inches. The sashed blocks are set on point with setting triangles. The sashing is 3 inches with 3-inch setting squares. The border uses two 3-inch strips with four pinwheel squares from the Shooting Star block.

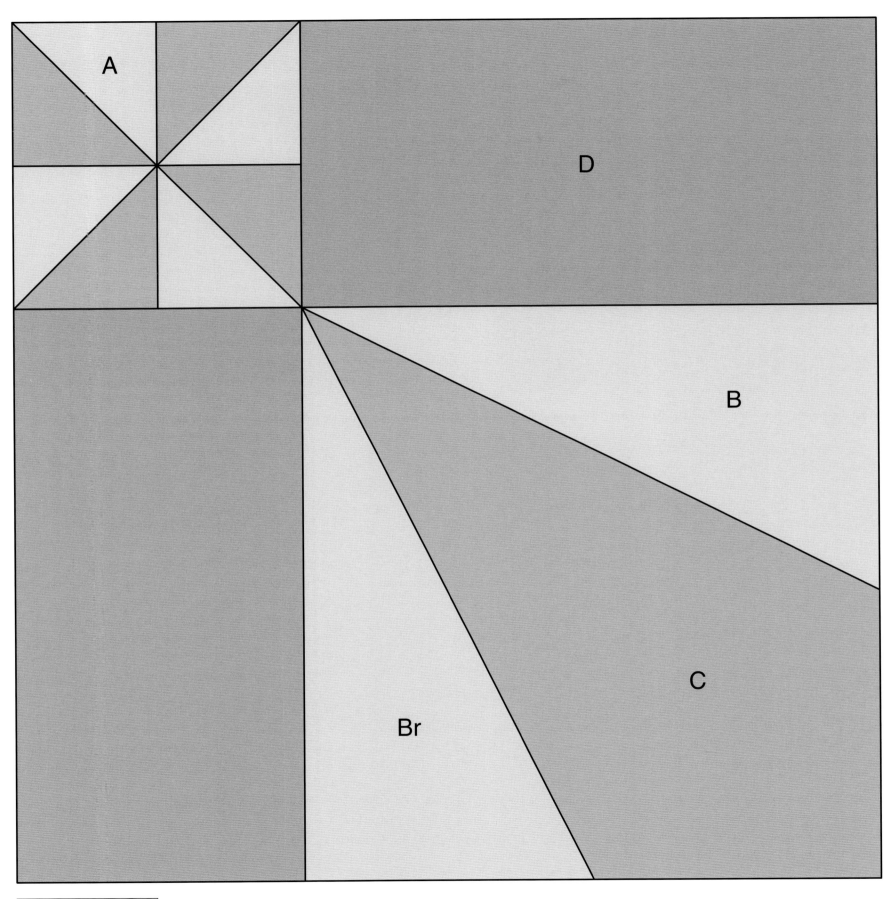

1920-1950 Fans

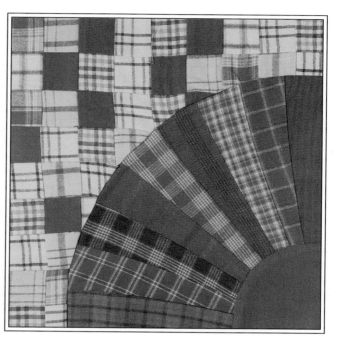

These blocks are inspired by the antique quilt on pages 144 and 145, bottom left.

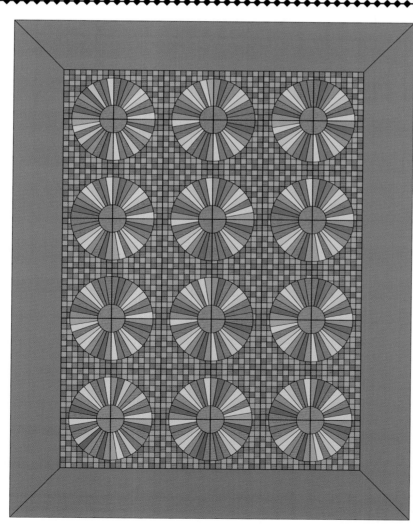

How to Construct This Block

Sew A to A (4 times). Sew AA to AA (2 times). Sew AAAA to AAAA; add A. Appliqué B to the A fan unit. Sew Cs together in nine rows each. Sew the rows together to make a background C unit. Appliqué the fan on the background C unit with neutral thread.

How to Make This Quilt

This quilt is designed to be a twin-size quilt measuring 72×90 inches, including a 9-inch border with mitered corners.

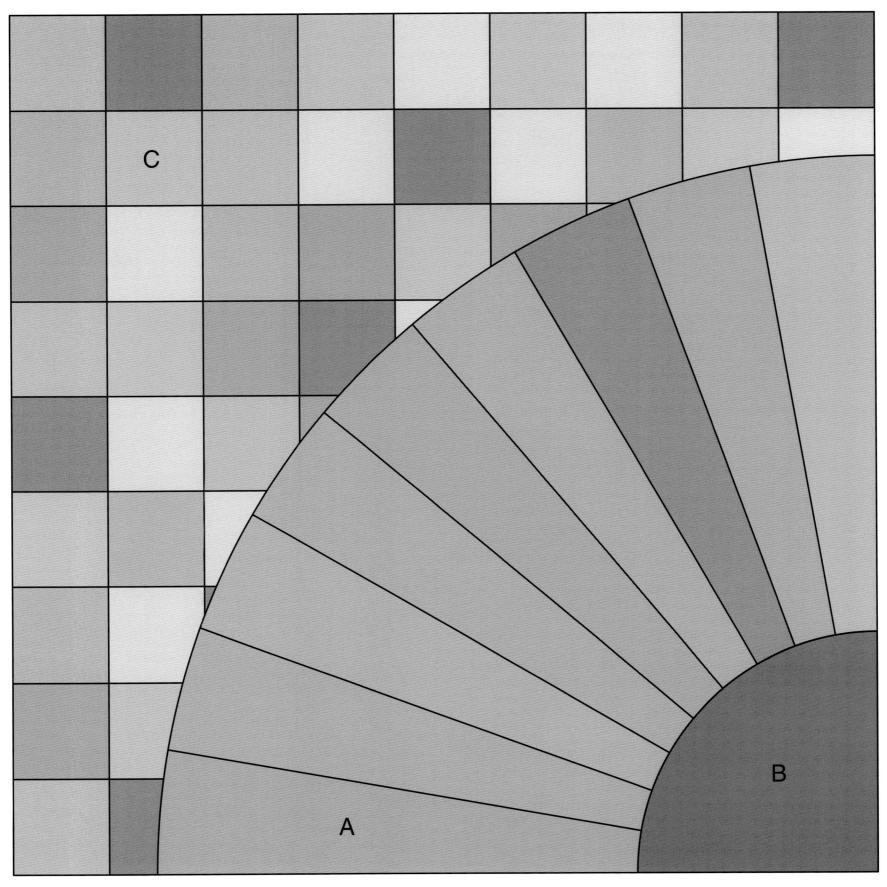

FANS
full-size block

These blocks are inspired by the antique quilt on page 149, bottom.

How to Construct This Block

Fold a 9½-inch background square diagonally twice; press. Cut 22—1½-inch circles to make 22 yo-yos for grapes. (See *page 199* to make yo-yos.) Beginning with A, lay out each pattern piece and pin in place. Unpin part of C and appliqué A. Appliqué the B and Br leaves in place, using matching threads. Appliqué stem C in place. Using the stitch diagrams on *page 199*, embroider vein lines on leaves, using a stem stitch and following the pattern markings. Add the yo-yos, following the placement lines to complete the block.

How to Make This Quilt

This quilt is designed to be a full-size quilt measuring 90×90 inches, including 9-inch setting squares.

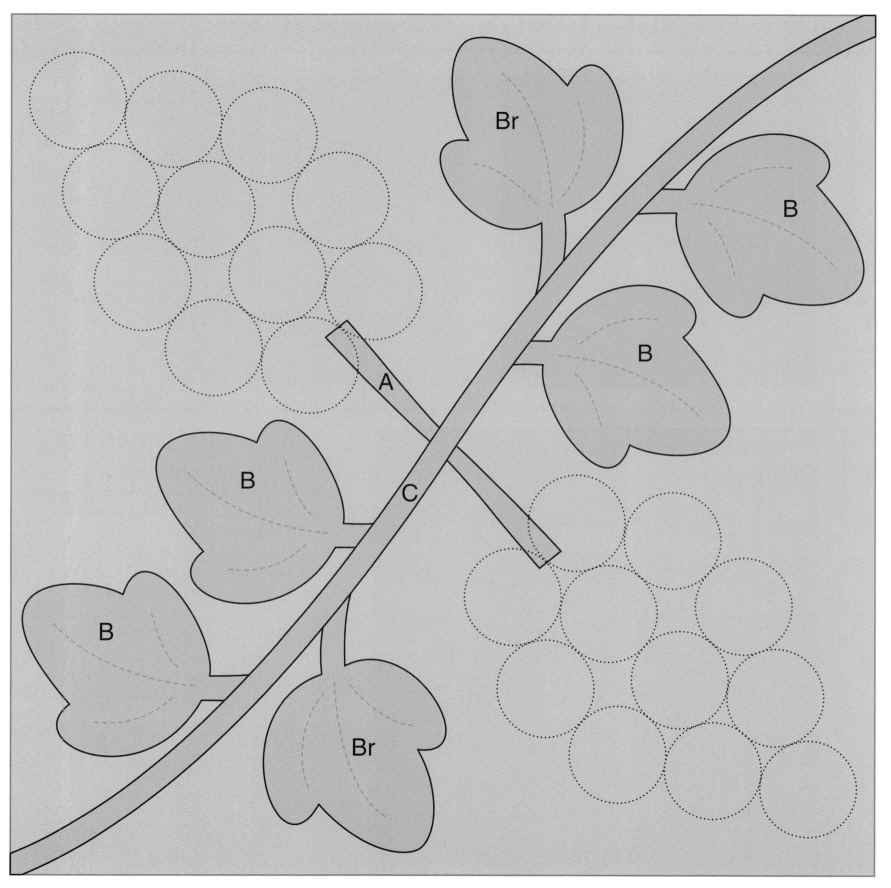

1920-1950 Postage Stamp

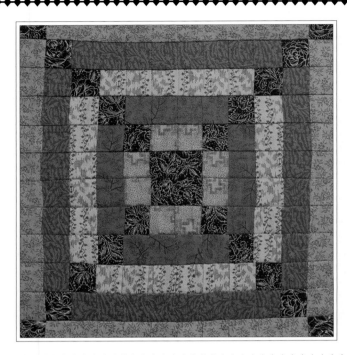

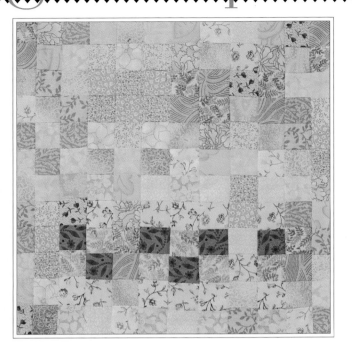

These blocks are inspired by the antique quilt on page 146, bottom.

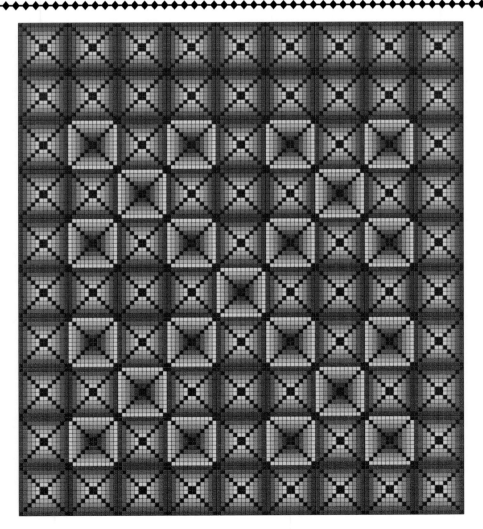

HOW TO CONSTRUCT THIS BLOCK

Assemble this block several different ways, as shown by the blocks, *above*, and the pattern, *opposite*. Option one, *above left*, creates an X. Option two, *above right*, has randomly placed squares. Option three, *opposite*, is arranged similar to the vintage quilt on *page 146*. Each block is created from 144 squares cut 1¼ inches. Lay out the As in a pleasing design with 12 squares in each row in a total of 12 rows. Sew 12 As together in each row, then join the rows to complete the block.

HOW TO MAKE THIS QUILT

This quilt is designed to be a full-size quilt measuring 81×90 inches using only blocks for this quilt top.

A

1920-1950 Embroidered Dresden

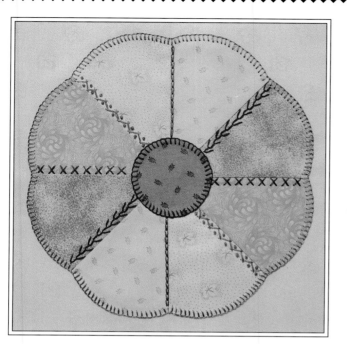
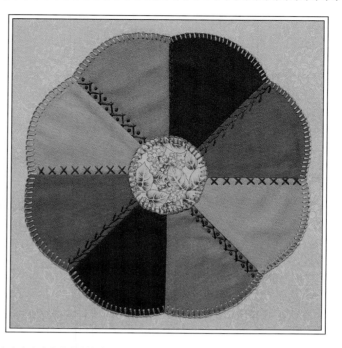

How to Construct This Block

Sew A to A (4 times). Sew AA to AA (2 times).
Sew AAAA to AAAA. Fold a 10-inch background square
in quarters, pressing the lines. Position the A unit onto
the background square, matching the seam lines to the
pressed lines of the square. Appliqué in place using
blanket stitches or other embroidery stitches (stitch
diagrams are on *page 199*), using matching threads.
Appliqué B to the center of the block. Trim the
background square to 9½ inches square.

How to Make This Quilt

This quilt is designed to be a full-size quilt measuring
81×99 inches, including a 4½-inch mitered inner border
and half-blocks with 4½-inch corner squares.

162

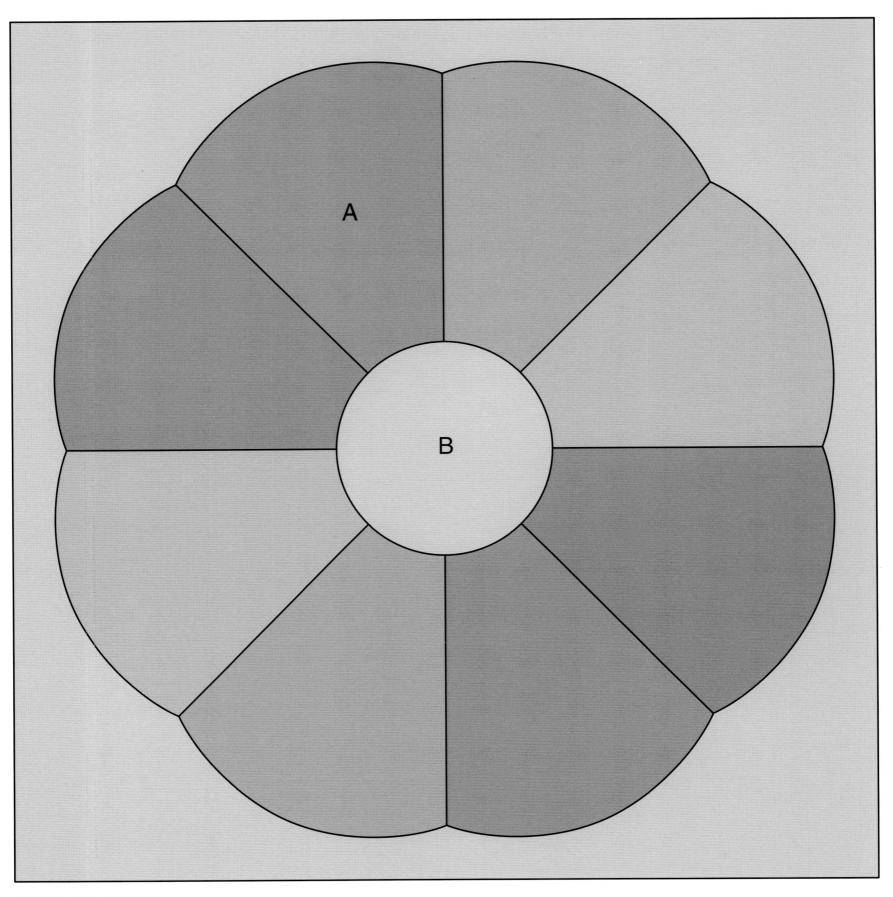

A

B

1920-1950 Fool's Puzzle

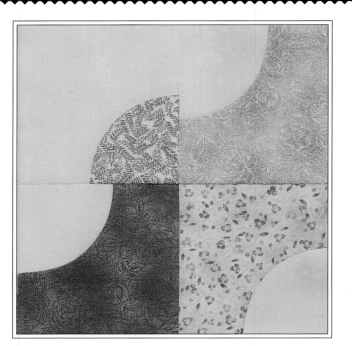

These blocks are inspired by the antique quilt on page 153.

HOW TO CONSTRUCT THIS BLOCK

To piece this block, mark the center of each A and B piece. Insert a pin at the center marks and ease the pieces to stitch them together. Sew a dark A to a light B. Sew a light A to a medium B. Sew a light A to a medium dark B. Sew a light A to a dark B. Sew AB to AB (2 times). Sew ABAB to ABAB.

To appliqué this block, cut B as a square; appliqué pattern A to B (4 times) using matching threads. Sew AB to AB (2 times). Sew ABAB to ABAB.

HOW TO MAKE THIS QUILT

This quilt is designed to be a king-size quilt measuring 112×112 inches, including a 2-inch border with mitered corners.

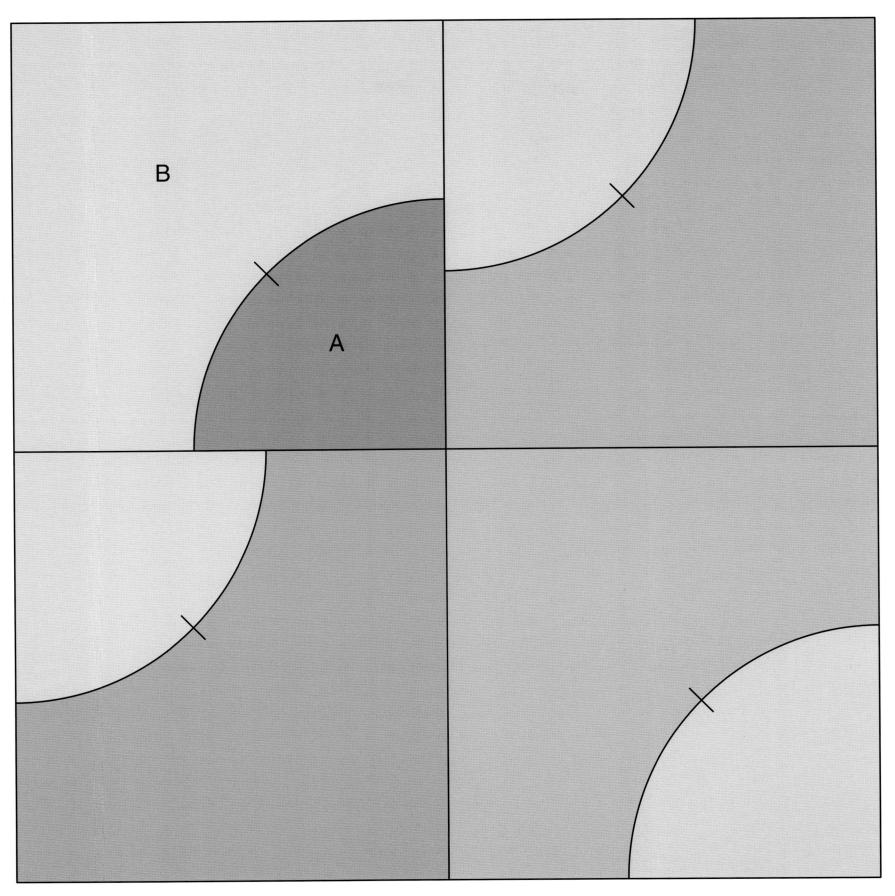

B

A

1920-1950 Poppies

These blocks are inspired by the antique quilt on page 145, bottom right.

How to Construct This Block

Fold a 10-inch background square diagonally twice in an X and press. Beginning with piece A, lay out each piece and pin in place, using the pressed lines as a placement guide. Using matching threads, appliqué each piece in alphabetical order. Trim the background square to measure 9½ inches square.

How to Make This Quilt

This quilt is designed to be a queen-size quilt measuring 90×108 inches, including a 9-inch inner border with corner blocks. The center section uses 18-inch plain corner squares. The outer border is 9 inches with corner blocks.

1920-1950 Sunbonnet Girls

These blocks are inspired by the antique quilt on page 150, top.

How to Construct This Block

Fold a 10-inch background square diagonally twice in an X and press. Lay out the appliqué pieces and pin in place, beginning with A. Appliqué each piece in order alphabetically with matching threads. Trim the background square to measure 9½ inches. The C and H pieces may be rickrack or other trim, if desired. Stem-stitch the feet with embroidery floss (see stitch diagram, *page 199*). Add buttons, lace, rickrack, or trims to embellish the clothing and hats of the Sunbonnet Girls.

How to Make This Quilt

This quilt is designed to be a twin-size quilt measuring 63×90 inches. Sunbonnet Girls, Sunbonnet Boys, and Alphabet Square blocks from *pages 88 and 213* are combined. The side and bottom borders are 9 inches. The top borders, above and below the lettering, are each 4½ inches.

These blocks are inspired by the antique quilt on page 150, top.

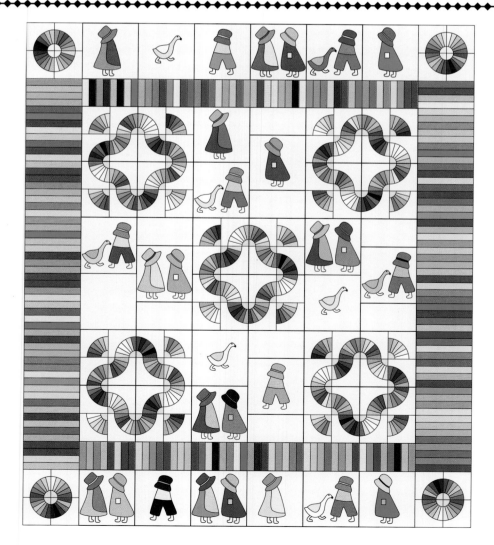

HOW TO CONSTRUCT THIS BLOCK

Fold a 10-inch background square diagonally twice in an X and press. Lay out and pin the appliqué pieces in place, beginning with A. Appliqué each piece in order alphabetically with matching threads. The D piece may be rickrack or other trim. Stem-stitch the feet and goose beak with embroidery floss (see stitch diagram, *page 199*). Fill in the beak with satin stitches. Trim the background square to measure 9½ inches.

HOW TO MAKE THIS QUILT

This quilt is designed to be a youth-size quilt measuring 72×81 inches. Sunbonnet Girl and Boy blocks are combined with Bunting blocks from *page 172* and squares and rectangles. The top and bottom striped border is made from 1⅛×4½-inch strips. The side borders are made from 1⅛×9-inch strips. The outer corners use four Bunting blocks.

1920-1950 Bunting

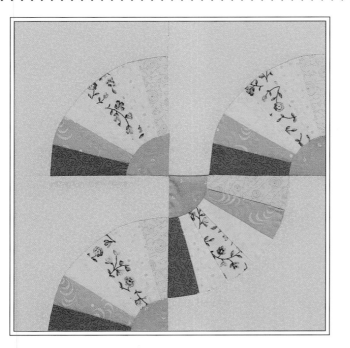

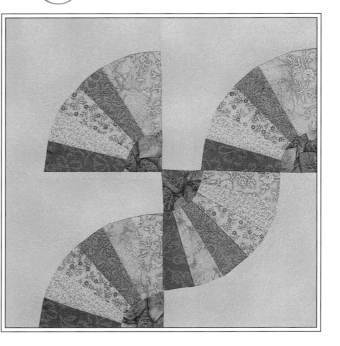

These blocks are inspired by the antique quilt on page 146, top.

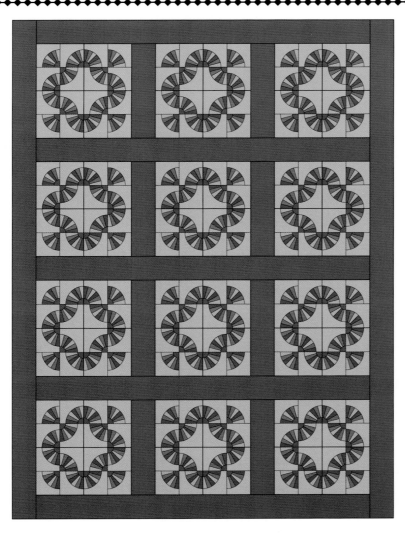

HOW TO CONSTRUCT THIS BLOCK

Unit 1: Sew light A to medium A (2 times). Sew dark A to AA (2 times). Sew AAA to AAA.

For remaining units: Sew dark A to medium A (6 times). Sew light A to AA (6 times). Sew AAA to AAA (3 times).

For all units: Appliqué A to C (4 times). Appliqué B to AC (4 times) to make a unit.

Following the pattern for placement, lay out four units in two rows. Sew the units together, then sew the rows together to complete the block.

HOW TO MAKE THIS QUILT

This quilt is designed to be a twin-size quilt measuring 72×94½ inches, including 4½-inch sashing and a 4½-inch border.

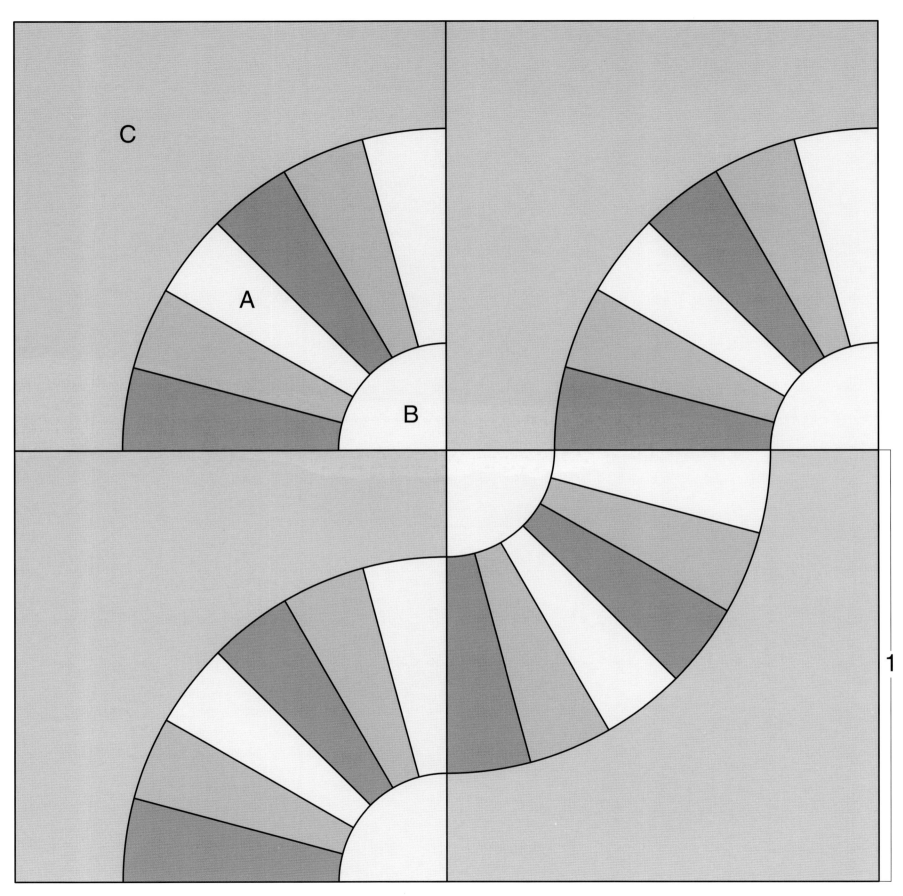

C

A

B

1

1920-1950 Cornucopia

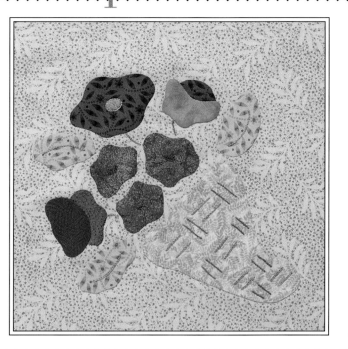

These blocks are inspired by the antique quilt on page 145, top.

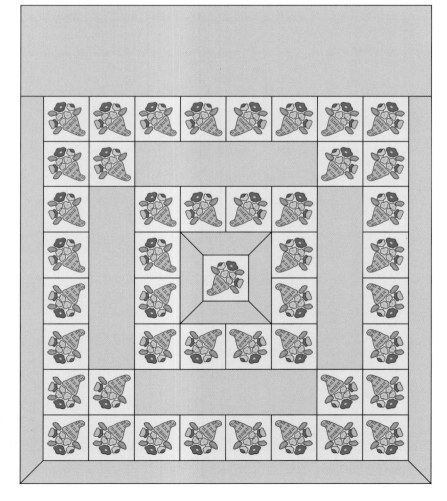

HOW TO CONSTRUCT THIS BLOCK

Fold a 10-inch background square diagonally twice in an X and press. Lay out the appliqué pieces and pin in place. Beginning with A, appliqué each piece in order alphabetically with matching threads. Trim the background square to measure 9½ inches. Using the diagrams on *page 199*, stem-stitch the leaf veins, cornucopia detail, and flower stems. The flower centers are satin-stitched with stem-stitch outline.

HOW TO MAKE THIS QUILT

This quilt is designed to be a twin- or full-size quilt measuring 81×94½ inches, including 4½-inch mitered sashing, and a 4½-inch mitered border on three sides. To serve as a pillow covering, the header is 18×81 inches.

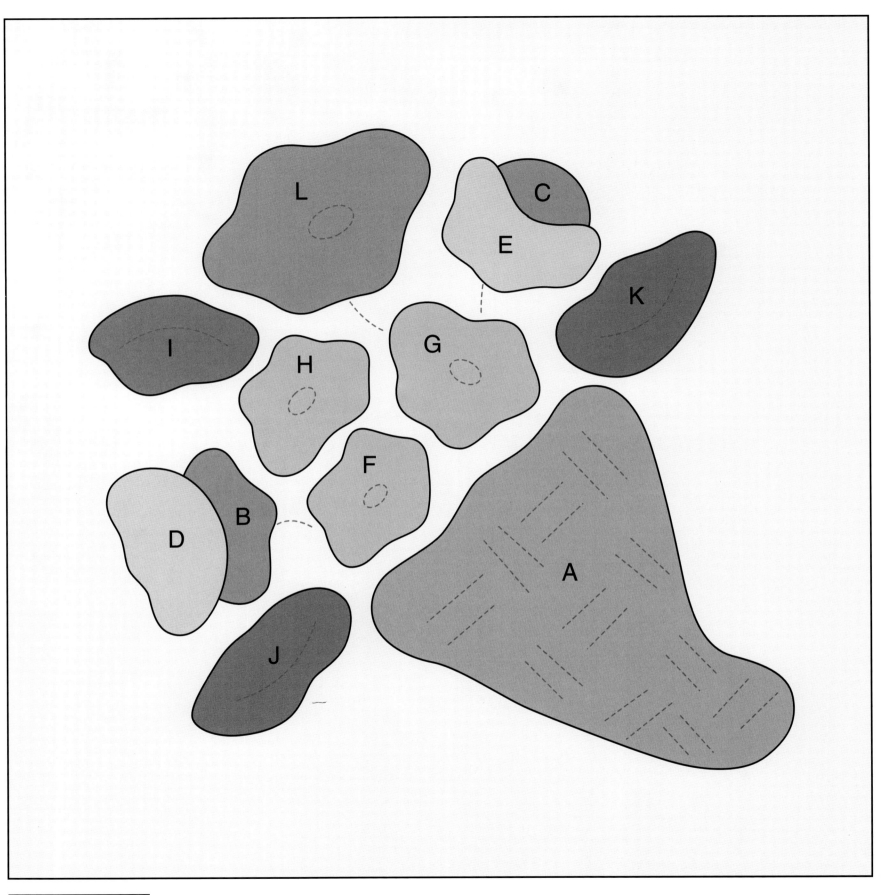

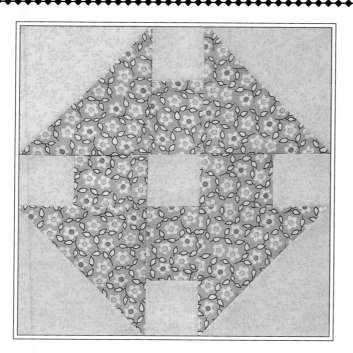

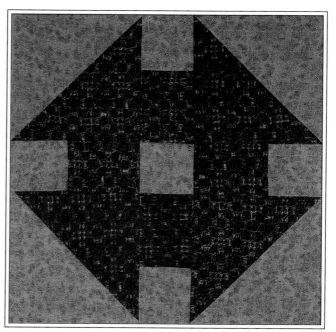

These blocks are inspired by the antique quilt on page 148.

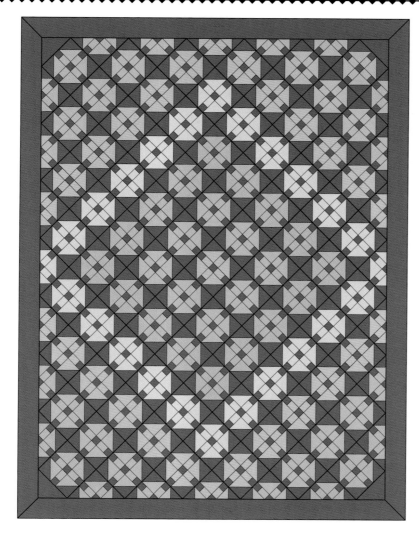

How to Construct This Block

Sew light A to dark A (4 times). Sew B to C (4 times). Sew one AA to BC. Sew AABC to AA to make top unit. Repeat for bottom unit. Sew BC to D. Sew BCD to BC to make center unit. Sew the three units together as shown.

How to Make This Quilt

This quilt is designed to be a queen-size quilt measuring 85½×111 inches. The blocks are set on point with half-blocks along the edges and setting triangles in the outside corners. The mitered border is 4½ inches.

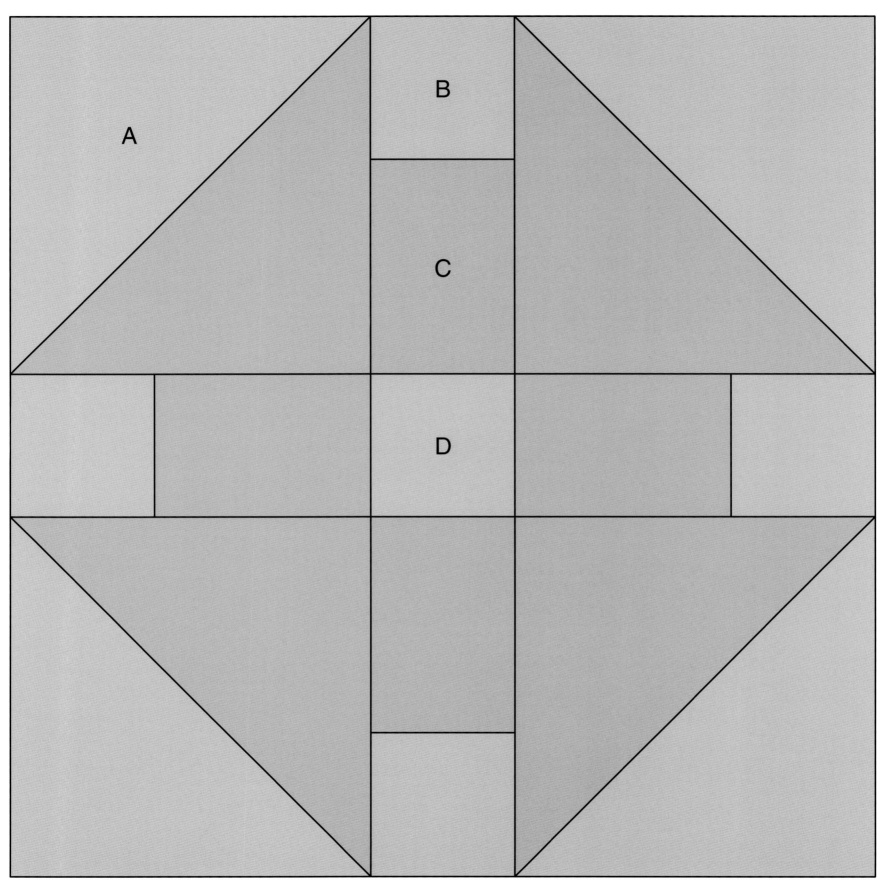

A

B

C

D

1920-1950 Resting Butterfly

These blocks are inspired by the antique quilt on page 148.

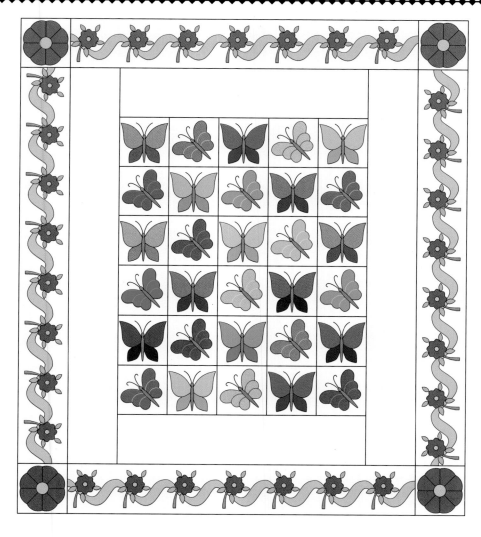

How to Construct This Block

Fold a 10-inch background square in quarters; press. Position A and B on background square and appliqué using contrasting embroidery floss and blanket stitches as shown on *page 199*. Appliqué C. Trim the background square to 9½ inches. Stem-stitch the antennae and work French knots at the ends.

How to Make This Quilt

This quilt is designed to be a full-size quilt measuring 81×90 inches, including a plain 9-inch inner border. The Resting Butterfly blocks are combined with the Butterfly in Flight blocks from *page 180*. The outer border is the Fancy Flower border from *page 210* with Embroidered Dresden blocks, *page 162*, in the corners.

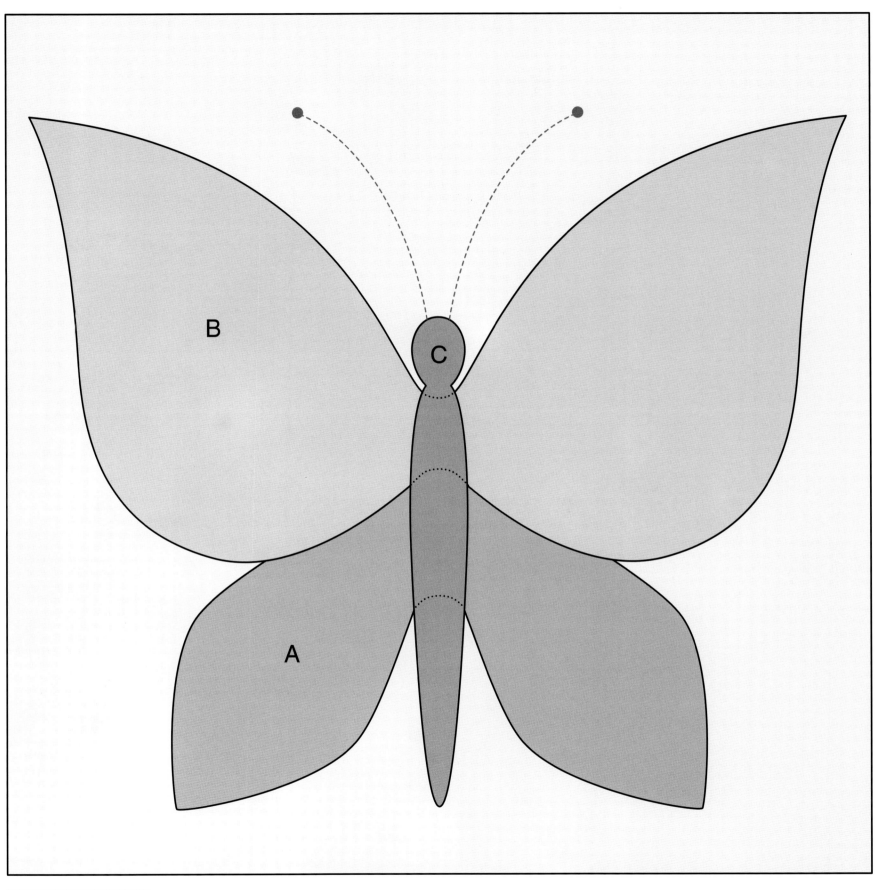

B

C

A

1920-1950 Butterfly in Flight

*These blocks are
inspired by the antique
quilt on page 148.*

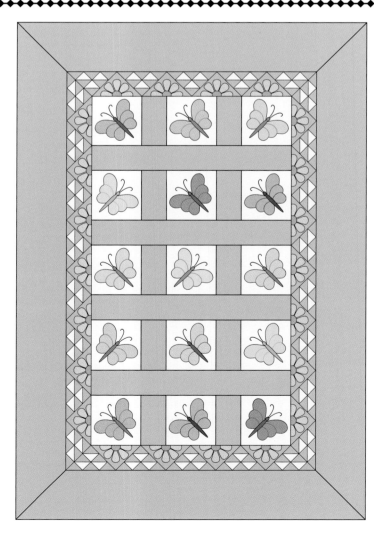

How to Construct This Block

Fold a 9½-inch background square diagonally twice
in an X; press. Appliqué A on the background square.
Appliqué B over A. Using the stitch diagrams on
page 199, embroider the wings and antennae using a
stem stitch. Blanket-stitch around the wings to complete
the block.

How to Make This Quilt

This quilt is designed to be a twin-size quilt measuring
63×90 inches, including 4½-inch sashing. The inner
border is the Daisy border from *page 207*. The outer
border is 9 inches wide with mitered corners.

A

B

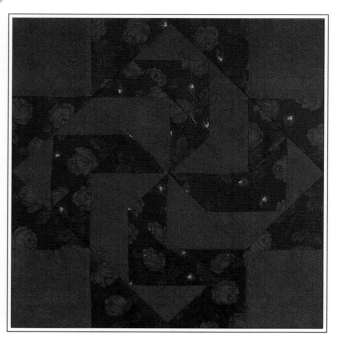

These blocks are inspired by the antique quilt on page 147.

HOW TO CONSTRUCT THIS BLOCK

Sew light A to each short side of dark B (4 times). Sew dark A to each short side of light B (4 times). Sew light ABA to the bottom of dark ABA (4 times). Noting placement, stitch ABAABA to ABAABA (2 times). Sew the two units together to make a center unit. Sew a light B to two adjoining sides of C (4 times). Sew one BCB to opposite sides of the center unit. Sew one BCB to each of the remaining sides of the center unit.

HOW TO MAKE THIS QUILT

This quilt is designed to be a twin-size quilt measuring 72×94½ inches, including the Flying Geese border from *page 209* and 4½-inch sashing squares.

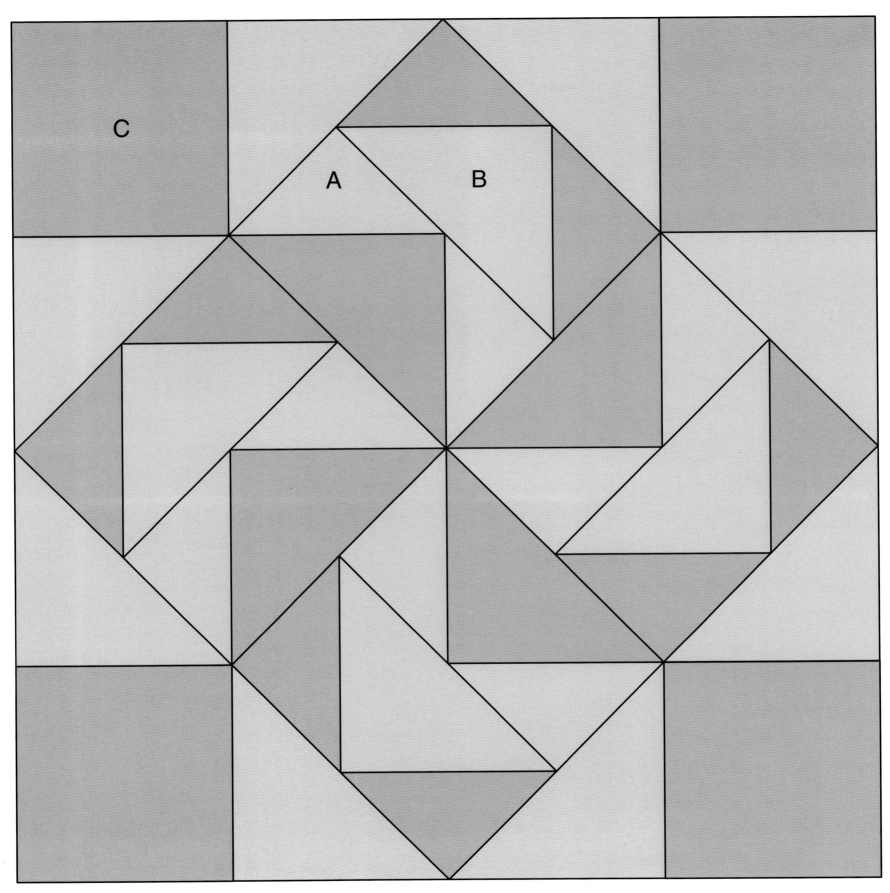

C

A   B

CRAZY ANN
full-size block

1920-1950 Prairie Queen

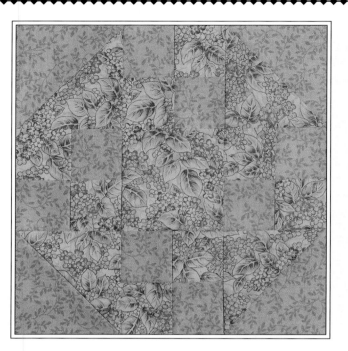 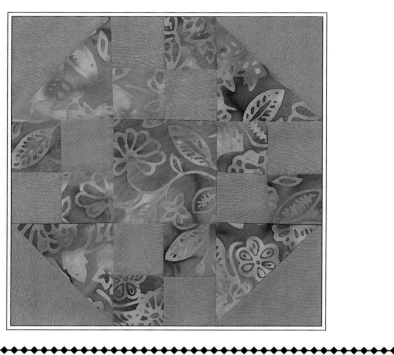

HOW TO CONSTRUCT THIS BLOCK

Sew light A to dark A (8 times). Sew AA to AA, reversing color placement (4 times). Sew light B to dark B (4 times). Sew BB to AAAA; add BB (2 times) for Rows 1 and 3. Sew AAAA to C; add AAAA for Row 2. Stitch Row 1 to Row 2; add Row 3.

HOW TO MAKE THIS QUILT

This quilt is designed to be a twin-size quilt measuring 72×90 inches. A variation of the Daisy border from *page 207* completes the quilt.

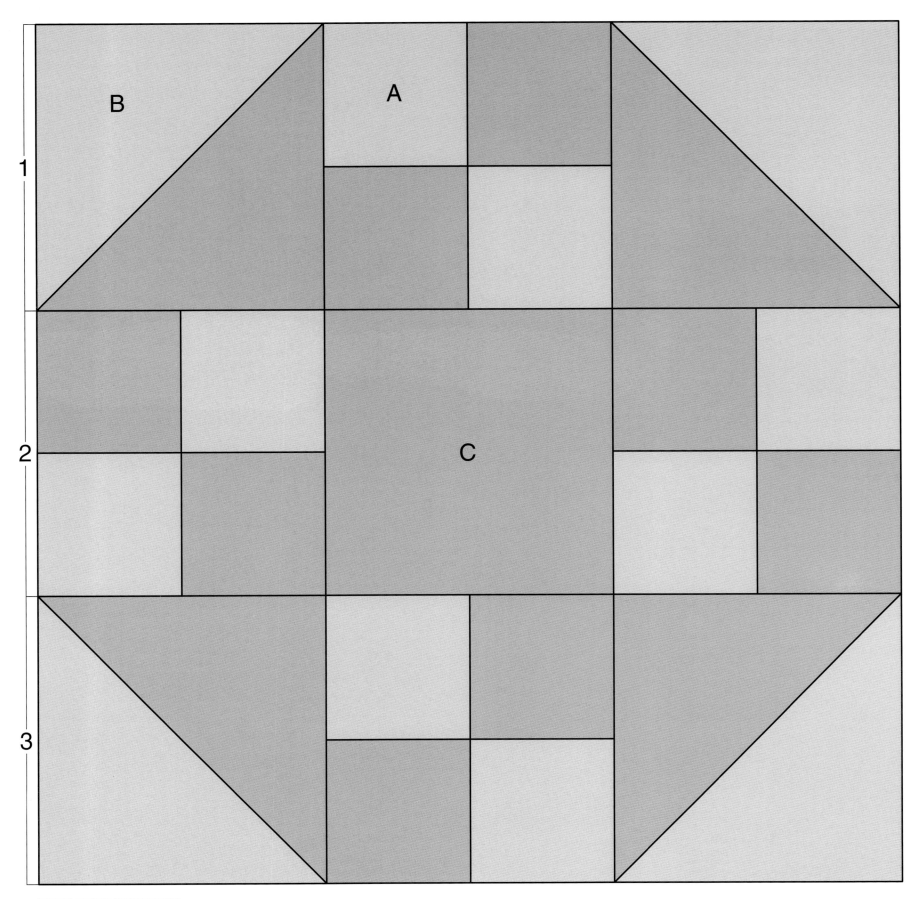

PRAIRIE QUEEN
full-size block

1920-1950 Ohio Rose

How to Construct This Block

Fold a 9½-inch background square diagonally twice in an X; press. Cut one 1½-inch circle and make a yo-yo flower center (see *page 199* to make yo-yos). Beginning with A, lay out each pattern piece and pin in place. Appliqué in place in alphabetical order. Sew the yo-yo to the center of the flower. Stitch five French knots at each bud tip to complete the block.

How to Make This Quilt

This quilt is designed to be a twin- or full-size quilt measuring 79½×92¼ inches. The blocks are set on point with plain blocks alternating between each Ohio Rose block. The Starry Scallop border, *page 212*, is used without the appliqué.

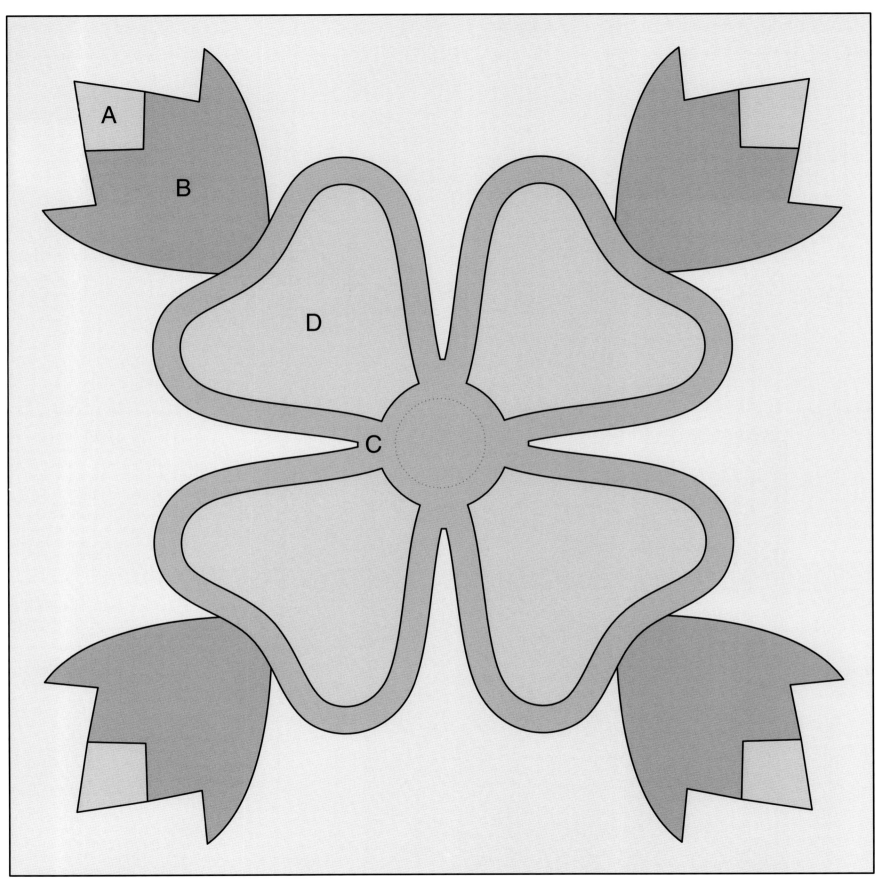

A

B

D

C

OHIO ROSE
full-size block

1920-1950 Shoo Fly

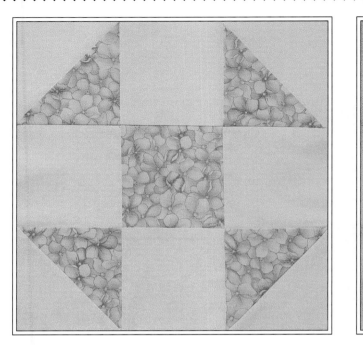 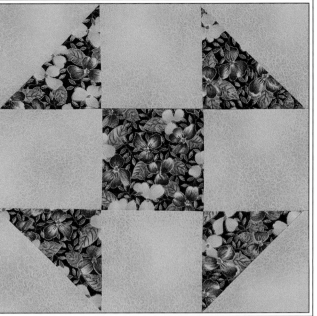

HOW TO CONSTRUCT THIS BLOCK

Sew A to A (4 times). Sew AA to opposite sides of B, being careful of placement (2 times) for Rows 1 and 3. Sew dark B to opposite sides of light B for Row 2. Sew Row 1 to Row 2; add Row 3.

HOW TO MAKE THIS QUILT

This quilt is designed to be a queen-size quilt measuring 95×112 inches. The blocks are set on point, and setting triangles form the inner border. The sashing consists of three 1-inch strips with 3-inch squares. The border is 3 inches wide.

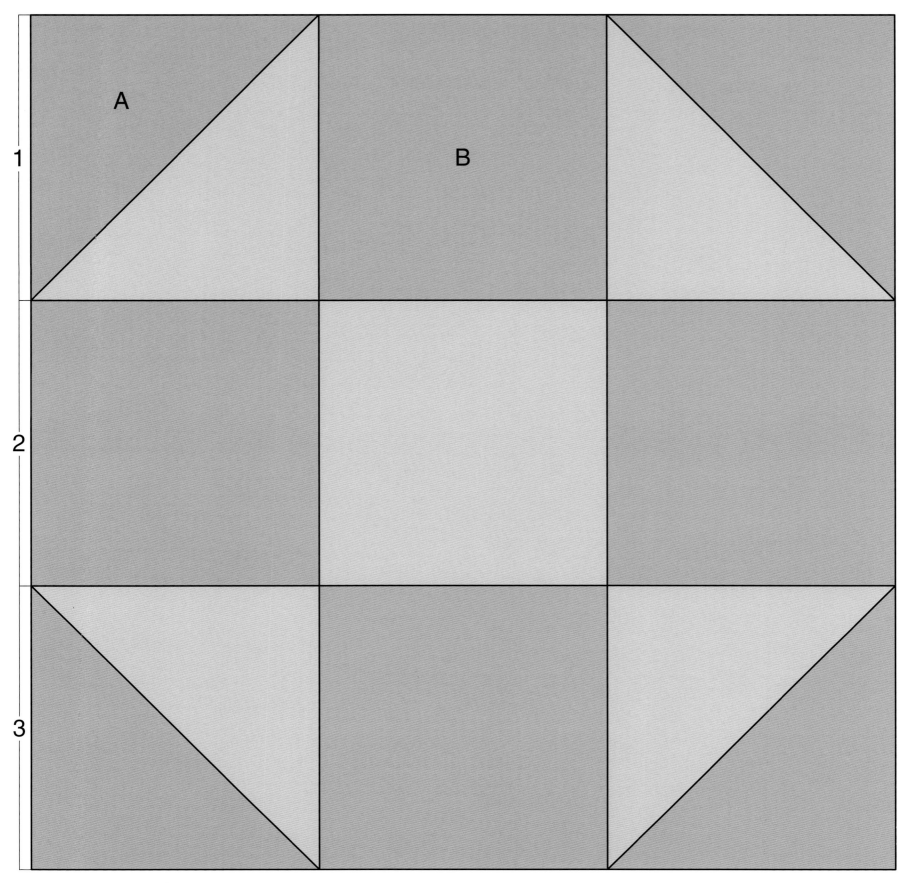

A

B

1

2

3

SHOO FLY
full-size block

1920-1950 Bow Tie

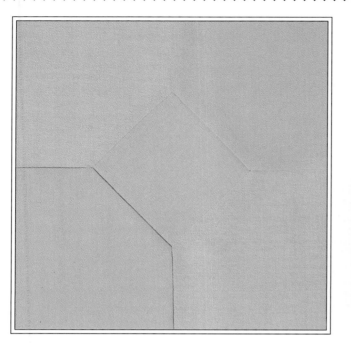

How to Construct This Block

Sew light A to opposite sides of B. Set in dark A to AB (2 times). Stop the stitching at the seam line of light AB. Reposition dark B and begin stitching at the seam line. Be careful not to stitch through the AB seam line. Stop the stitching at the next light AB seam line, reposition the dark B and begin stitching at the seam line.

How to Make This Quilt

This quilt is designed to be a full- or queen-size quilt measuring 90×99 inches, including a 4½-inch inner border. The outer border is made of three rows of 4½-inch squares set in checkerboard fashion as shown.

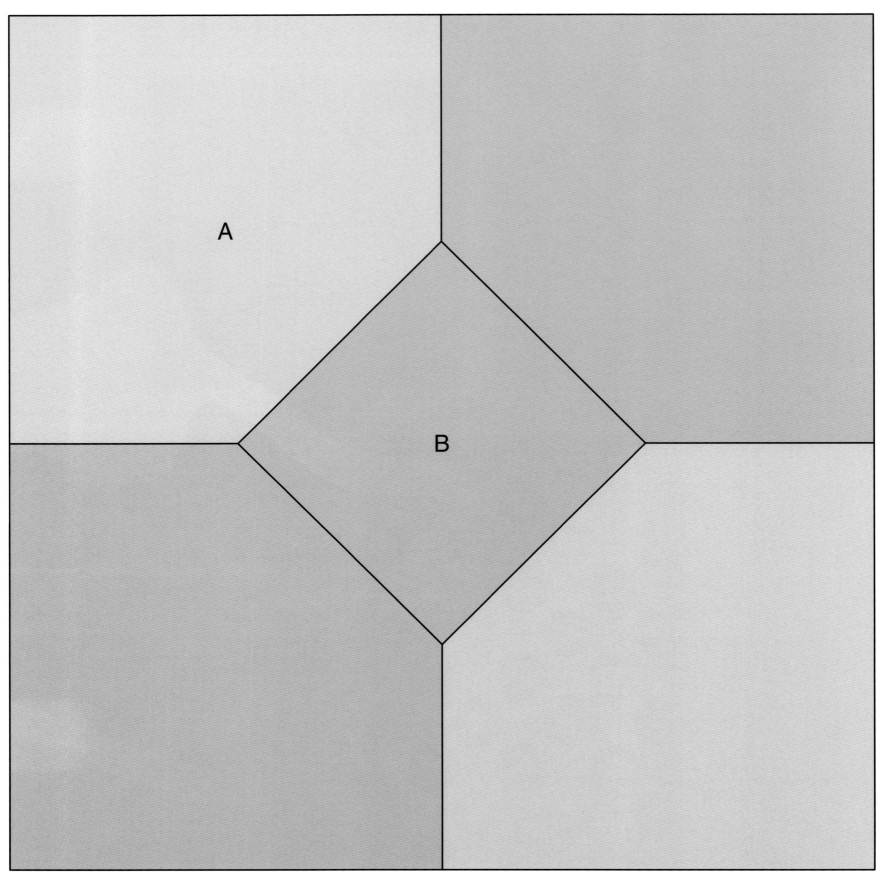

A

B

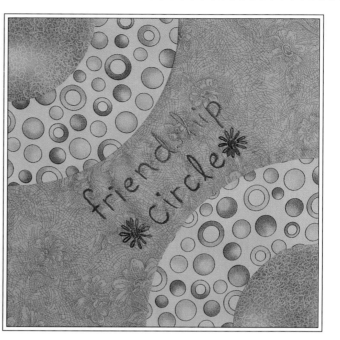

These blocks are inspired by the antique quilt on page 150, bottom.

HOW TO CONSTRUCT THIS BLOCK

This block may be pieced or appliquéd.

To piece:
Transfer the placement marks to the templates and mark each fabric piece with the placement marks. Pin two pieces together, matching marks. Ease the pieces together while sewing. Sew A to B (2 times). Sew AB to C (2 times).

To appliqué:
Appliqué B (2 times) to a 9½-inch C background square. Appliqué A to BC (2 times).

Using the stitch diagrams on *page 199*, stem-stitch *friendship circle* or other words in the center of the block. Stitch lazy daisy stitches on both sides. If desired, fabric markers may be used for signatures.

HOW TO MAKE THIS QUILT

This quilt is designed to be a twin-size quilt measuring 63×99 inches, including the Zigzag border from *page 204* with 4½-inch corners.

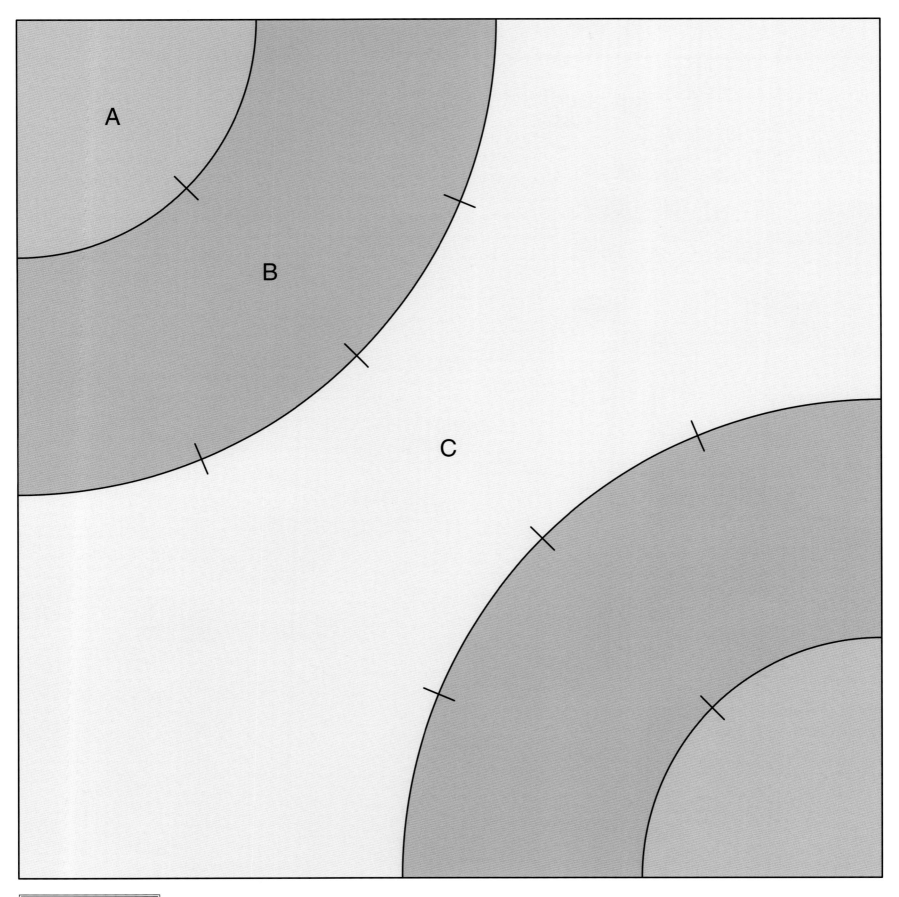

A

B

C

SIGNATURE CIRCLES
full-size block

Quilt How-to

CRAZY ANN QUILT

Pictured on page 147.

MATERIALS

6 yards of white fabric
3¼ yards of blue fabric
5⅓ yards of backing fabric
77×105-inch piece of quilt batting

Finished quilt: 70⅝×98⅞ inches
Finished quilt block: 10 inches square
    Quantities specified are for
44/45-inch-wide 100 percent cotton
fabrics. All measurements include a ¼-inch
seam allowance unless otherwise specified.

CUT THE FABRIC

To make the best use of fabrics, cut the
pieces in the following order.
From white fabric, cut:
70—8-inch squares, cutting each in half
    diagonally for a total of 140 setting triangles
210—3⅜-inch squares, cutting each in
    half diagonally for a total of 420 large
    triangles, or 420 of Pattern B
140—2⅝-inch squares, cutting each in
    half diagonally for a total of 280 small
    triangles, or 280 of Pattern A

From blue fabric, cut:
74—3⅜-inch squares, cutting each in half
    diagonally for a total of 148 large
    triangles, or 148 of Pattern B
136—3-inch squares or 136 of Pattern C
140—2⅝-inch squares, cutting each in
    half diagonally for a total of 280 small
    triangles, or 280 of Pattern A
9—2½×42-inch binding strips

MAKE THE BLOCKS

For one Crazy Ann block you will need
8 white A triangles, 12 white B triangles,
8 blue A triangles, 4 blue B triangles, and
4 blue C squares. Follow the piecing
directions on *page 182*. Complete
33 full-size Crazy Ann blocks.

MAKE THE HALF-BLOCK

1. For one Crazy Ann half-block you will
   need 4 white A triangles, 6 white
   B triangles, 4 blue A triangles, 4 blue
   B triangles, and 1 blue C square.
2. Follow the directions given to make
   the 9-inch Crazy Ann block on *page 182*,
   completing construction layout as
   shown in Diagram 1, *below*. Trim
   the half-block to measure
   short sides 10½ inches and
   long sides 14½ inches,
   including seam
   allowances.
   Repeat to
   make four
   half-blocks.

Crazy Ann
Pattern A

Crazy Ann
Pattern B

Crazy Ann
Pattern C

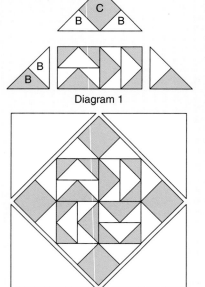

Diagram 1

Diagram 2

Quilt Assembly Diagram

ADD THE SETTING TRIANGLES

Sew white setting triangles to opposite sides of a block (Diagram 2, *opposite*). Press the seam allowances toward the triangles. Repeat to complete all 33 full-size blocks. Press the seam allowances toward the triangles. The block should measure 14⅝ inches, including seam allowances. Sew two white setting triangles to the short side of each Crazy Ann half block; press the seam allowance toward the triangles.

ASSEMBLE THE QUILT TOP

Referring to the Quilt Assembly Diagram *above*, lay out the 33 Crazy Ann blocks and the 4 half-blocks in five vertical rows. Sew together the blocks in each vertical row. Press the seam allowances in alternating directions in each row. Join the rows to complete the quilt top. Press all seam allowances in one direction.

COMPLETE THE QUILT

1. Layer the quilt top, batting, and backing. Quilt as desired.
2. Bind the quilt using the blue binding strips.

BUTTERFLY QUILT

Pictured on page 148.

MATERIALS

5—9-inch squares of print fabrics
1¼ yards of white for blocks, setting squares, and inner border
1½ yards of blue-and-white print for outer border and backing
¼ yard of solid blue for binding
39×43-inch piece of quilt batting

Finished quilt size: 32½×37 inches
Finished quilt block: 9½ inches square
  Quantities specified are for
44/45-inch-wide 100 percent cotton fabrics. All measurements include a ¼-inch seam allowance unless otherwise specified.

CUT THE FABRIC

To make the best use of fabrics, cut the pieces in the following order.
From white, cut:
5—10-inch foundation squares
4—9½-inch squares
2—2×32½-inch border strips (#2)
2—3×27½-inch border strips (#1)
From blue-and-white print, cut:
2—1¾×37½-inch border strips (#4)
2—3×30½-inch border strips (#3)
1—39×43-inch backing
From solid blue, cut:
4—2×42-inch strips for binding

APPLIQUÉ THE BUTTERFLY BLOCKS

For each butterfly block, you will need one white 10-inch foundation square and one 9-inch piece of print fabric. Follow the directions given for the block that you are making from *pages 178–181*. Make two Resting Butterfly blocks and three Butterfly in Flight blocks. Trim each block to 9½ inches square including seam allowances.

ASSEMBLE THE QUILT CENTER

Referring to the Quilt Assembly Diagram, *left*, lay out the five completed blocks and four setting squares in three horizontal rows. Sew together the blocks in each row. Join the rows. The pieced quilt center should measure 27½ inches square.

continued on page 196

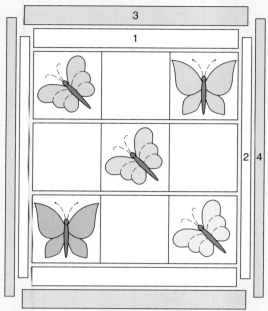

Quilt Assembly Diagram

Border Corner Cutting Guide

ADD INNER BORDER

Sew one 3×27½-inch white border (#1) to the top and bottom of the quilt center. Sew a 2×32½-inch white border (#2) to each side of the quilt center. Press seam allowances toward the border strips.

ADD OUTER BORDER

Sew one 3×30½-inch blue-and-white print border (#3) to the top and bottom of the quilt center. Sew a 1¾×37½-inch blue-and-white print border (#4) to each side of the quilt center. Press the seam allowances toward the border strips.

COMPLETE THE QUILT

1. This quilt has rounded corners. To duplicate this look, use the pattern at *left* or trace around a plate and then mark and cut the curve after all borders have been added.

2. Layer the quilt top, batting, and backing. This quilt was quilted by machine, using 1-inch-wide squares nested inside one another in the setting squares and 1¼ inch in on butterfly squares. Diagonal lines from corner to corner and the borders were machine stitched with straight lines. Bind the quilt with the solid blue strips.

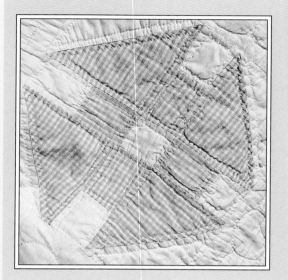

CHURN DASH QUILT

Pictured on page 148.

MATERIALS

⅜ yard each of gold check, light green solid, and blue check for blocks

¼ yard each of pink check and dark blue, peach, tan, and pink solid for blocks

3⅛ yards of white for setting squares, and side, and corner triangles

2⅜ yards of light peach solid for borders and binding

4 yards of backing fabric

72×83-inch piece of quilt batting

Finished quilt: 66×77 inches
Finished block: 7¾ inches square
  Quantities specified are for 44/45-inch-wide 100 percent cotton fabrics. All measurements include a ¼-inch seam allowance unless otherwise specified.

CUT THE FABRIC

To make the best use of fabrics, cut the pieces in the following order. The border and binding strips are cut parallel to the selvage of the fabric. For this project, the setting and corner triangles are cut larger than necessary to allow for sewing differences. After assembling the quilt center, trim them to fit. The listings include the mathematically correct border lengths. You may wish to add extra length to the borders to allow for sewing differences. Trim the border strips to the actual length before adding them to the quilt top.

From each gold check and light green solid, cut:

12—4⅛-inch squares, cutting each in half diagonally for a total of 24 triangles, or 24 of Pattern A

24—1¾×2⅛-inch rectangles, or 24 of Pattern C

From blue check, cut:

10—4⅛-inch squares, cutting each in half diagonally for a total of 20 triangles, or 20 of Pattern A

20—1¾×2⅛-inch rectangles or 20 of Pattern C

From pink check, cut:

8—4⅛-inch squares, cutting each in half diagonally for a total of 16 triangles, or 16 of Pattern A

16—1¾×2⅛-inch rectangles or 16 of Pattern C

From each dark blue and peach, cut:

6—4⅛-inch squares, cutting each in half diagonally for a total of 12 triangles, or 12 of Pattern A

12—1¾×2⅛-inch rectangles or 12 of Pattern C

From tan, cut:

4—4⅛-inch squares, cutting each in half diagonally for a total of 8 triangles, or 8 of Pattern A

8—1¾×2⅛-inch rectangles or 8 of Pattern C

From pink solid, cut:

2—4⅛-inch squares, cutting each in half diagonally for a total of 4 triangles, or 4 of Pattern A

4—1¾×2⅛-inch rectangles or 4 of Pattern C

From white, cut:

5—12½-inch squares, cutting each diagonally twice in an X for a total of 20 setting triangles (you'll use 18)

20—8¼-inch squares for setting squares

2—6½-inch squares, cutting each in half diagonally for a total of 4 corner triangles

60—4⅛-inch squares, cutting each in half diagonally for a total of 120 triangles, or 120 of Pattern A

120—1¾×2⅛-inch rectangles or 120 of Pattern B

30—1¾-inch squares, or 30 of Pattern D

continued on page 198

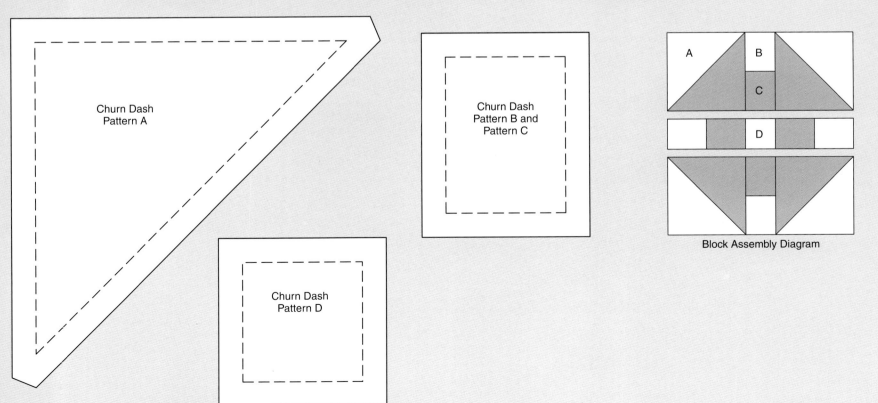

Churn Dash Pattern A

Churn Dash Pattern B and Pattern C

Churn Dash Pattern D

Block Assembly Diagram

197

Quilt Assembly Diagram

From light peach solid, cut:
2—6×77½-inch border strips (#2)
2—6×55½-inch border strips (#1)
4—2×78-inch strips for binding

ASSEMBLE THE BLOCKS

For one block you will need four white
A triangles, four white B rectangles, and
one white D square. In the same print
you'll need four A triangles and four
C rectangles. Following the piecing
directions on *page 176*, complete a total
of 30 blocks.

ASSEMBLE THE QUILT TOP

1. Referring to the photograph, *page 148*,
   or Quilt Assembly Diagram, *above*, lay
   out the Churn Dash blocks, 20 white
   8¼-inch setting squares, and 18 white
   setting triangles in diagonal rows. The
   corner triangles will be added later.
2. Sew together the pieces in each
   diagonal row. Press the seam allowances
   toward the white setting squares and
   triangles. Join the rows. Add the four
   white corner triangles. Press all seam
   allowances in one direction.
3. Trim the setting and corner triangles to
   leave a ¼-inch seam allowance beyond
   the block corners. The pieced quilt
   center should measure 55½×66½
   inches, including seam allowances.

ADD THE BORDERS

1. Before cutting borders, measure the quilt
   top and adjust the lengths to fit. Sew one
   peach 6×55½-inch border strip (#1) to
   the top and bottom edges of the pieced
   quilt center. Add one peach 6×77½-inch
   border strip (#2) to each side edge of the
   quilt top.
2. Press the seam allowances toward the
   borders.

COMPLETE THE QUILT

1. Layer the quilt top, batting, and
   backing. Quilt as desired. The original
   quiltmaker hand-quilted the setting
   blocks with a feathered wreath,
   outlined the pieces in the quilt block
   ¼ inch in from the seams, and used
   an oval interlocking chain pattern for
   the borders.
2. Bind the quilt with the 2×78-inch
   black strips.

Stitch Diagrams

Appliqué Stitch

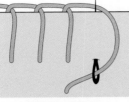

Blanket Stitch

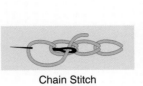

Chain Stitch

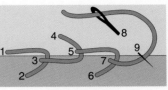

Cross-Stitch

Featherstitch

French Knot

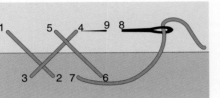

Herringbone

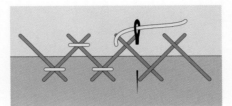

Herringbone with Couching

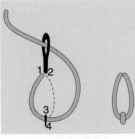

Lazy Daisy Stitch

Satin Stitch

Smyrna-Cross Variation

Stem Stitch

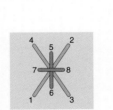

Straight Stitch

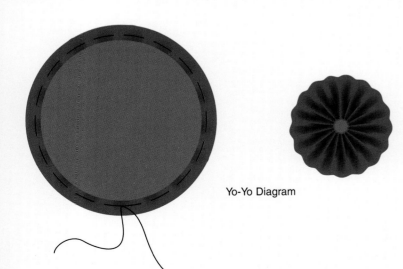

Yo-Yo Diagram

Yo-Yos

To determine the cutting size of the yo-yo piece, determine the finished size of the yo-yo and double the diameter. For example, for a 1-inch yo-yo, draw a 2-inch circle and add ¼- to ½-inch seam allowance.

To make several yo-yos the same size, make a plastic template. Trace the template onto fabric, mark three or four layers of fabric, and cut several yo-yo circles at once. The sharper the scissors, the more fabric layers can be cut at a time.

To sew yo-yos, use quilting thread and knot the end. Turn under a scant ¼ inch and work running stitches close to the folded edge. (Avoid tiny stitches, which put too many gathers in the circle and make the hole too big.) End where you began, bringing the needle through the fabric to the side without the cut edge. Pull the thread firmly to draw the yo-yo closed. Tack with a few stitches to secure.

Borders

꧁

The edges of quilts are sewn in a variety of ways. Many early quilts had binding to hold the layers together and provide a finished edge. As quilt patterns emerged and quilting skills were honed, quilts showcased elaborate pieced and appliquéd borders. The borders in this chapter are inspired by vintage quilts and include delicate florals, bold geometrics, and starry scallops.

About Borders

Borders form the horizontal and vertical edges of fabric stitched on a quilt top to frame the finished design. Not all quilts have borders. On many, particularly those with overall repeat designs, the pattern extends to the binding. Amish quilt designs, on the other hand, often feature two or three broad borders in different colors, one set within the other, making an effective frame for a center medallion design. The borders of Amish quilts traditionally are not mitered.

Elegant appliqué quilts designed during the 19th century often featured curved edges or scalloped borders to showcase the glorious work.

Occasionally, the top border of the quilt was made very wide so it would be featured as it lay across the pillows at the head of the bed.

All of the borders in this chapter have 9-inch repeats, with the exception of the Prairie Point, making them easy to use with any of the quilt blocks or assembly diagrams in the book.

FANCY FLOWER BORDER
c.1850s

(ABOVE) FROM THE ALBUM QUILT ON PAGE 12 COMES THIS APPLIQUÉD FLORAL BORDER. THE FLOWING ZIGZAG APPEARS AS RIBBON. PATTERNS AND INSTRUCTIONS FOR THIS BORDER BEGIN ON PAGE 210.
Courtesy: University of Nebraska-Lincoln

STARRY SCALLOP BORDER
c.1900

(RIGHT) THIS PATRIOTIC BORDER SERVES AS A SHOWY FINALE ON THIS EMBROIDERED BLOCK STATE QUILT. PATTERNS AND INSTRUCTIONS FOR THIS BORDER ARE ON PAGE 212.
Courtesy: Dianne Handley

PRAIRIE POINTS BORDER
c.1930

(OPPOSITE) THIS QUILT SHOWS A WONDERFUL EXAMPLE OF A PRAIRIE POINTS BORDER. THE MAKER USED A DIFFERENT FABRIC FOR EACH POINT. INSTRUCTIONS FOR MAKING PRAIRIE POINTS ARE ON PAGE 210.
Courtesy: Jill Price

DIAMOND BORDER
c.1860

(BELOW) THIS STRIKING GEOMETRIC DIAMOND BORDER FRAMES THE NEW YORK BEAUTY QUILT SHOWN ON PAGE 66. THE SASHING STRIPS INSPIRED THE SAWTOOTH BORDER ON THE NEXT PAGE. PATTERNS AND INSTRUCTIONS FOR THESE BORDERS ARE ON PAGES 202–203.
Courtesy: University of Nebraska-Lincoln

Sawtooth

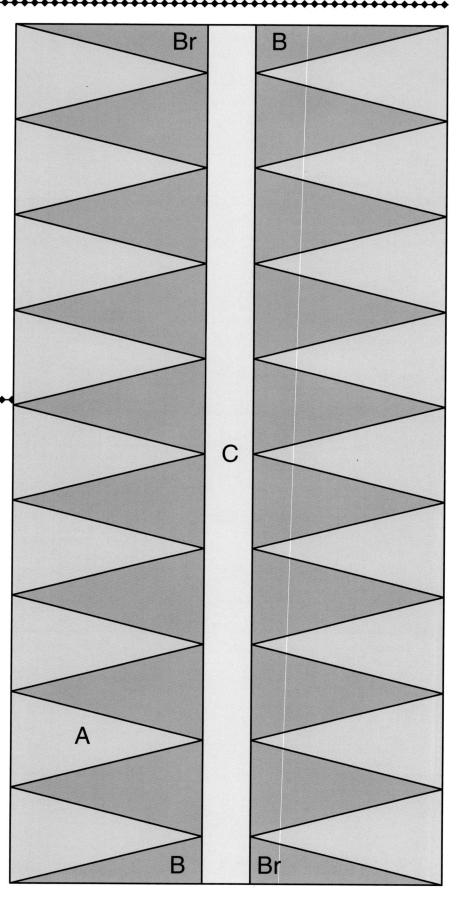

HOW TO CONSTRUCT THIS BORDER

This border is inspired by the sashing strips from the bottom quilt on page 201.

Sew light A to dark A (16 times). Sew AA to AA
(8 times). Sew AAAA to AAAA (4 times). Sew 2
AAAAAAAA units together to make each side.
Position the units to mirror each other. Sew B to the
left side of each unit. Sew A to the left side of Br (2
times). Sew ABr to the right side of each unit. Follow
the pattern diagram, *right,* to reverse positions of the
units to mirror each other. Sew the dark bottom side
of each unit to the long side of C, being careful to
match up points on the opposite side.

SAWTOOTH
full-size border

Diamond

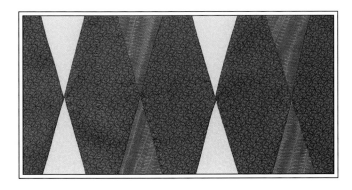

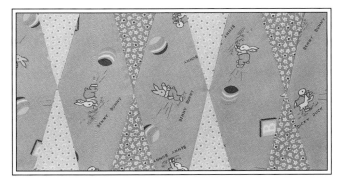

HOW TO CONSTRUCT THIS BORDER

This border is inspired by the New York Beauty antique quilt on page 66.

To opposite sides of A, sew light B and medium B (3 times). Reversing color positions, sew BAB to BAB. Add BAB to make one unit. Sew light B to the top right side of C. Sew medium B to the bottom left side of C. Following the pattern, *right,* for placement, sew BC to each side of the unit, reversing color placement.

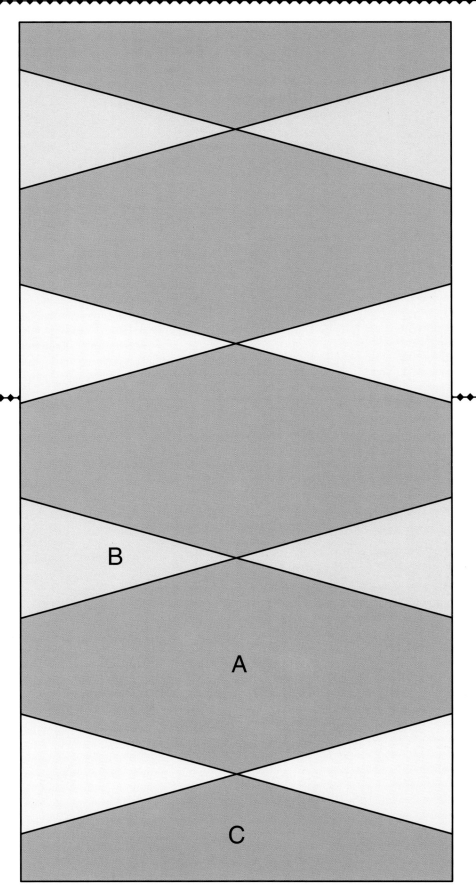

Zigzag

HOW TO CONSTRUCT THIS BORDER

This border is inspired by the Ships of Maine antique quilt on page 11.

Sew light A to dark A (7 times). Sew AA to AA
(3 times). Sew AAAA to AA to make Row 1.
Sew AAAA to AAAA to make Row 2. Sew dark B to
light C. Sew light B to dark C. Sew dark BC to
AAAAAA; add BC to make Row 1. Sew Row 1 to
Row 2.

ZIGZAG
full-size border

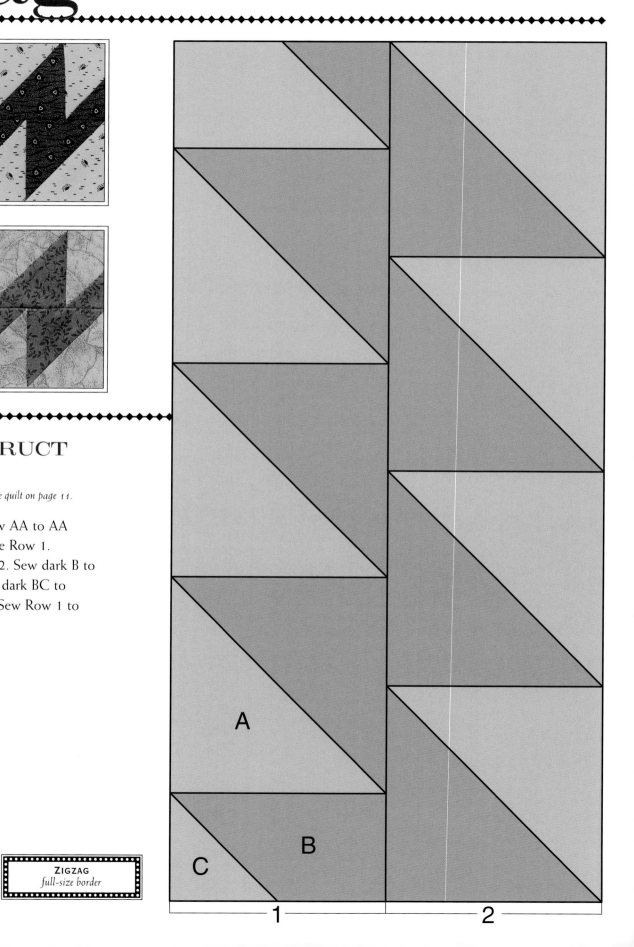

204

Diamond Link

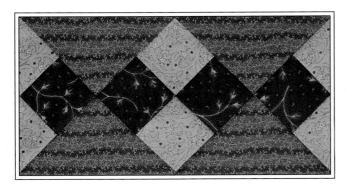

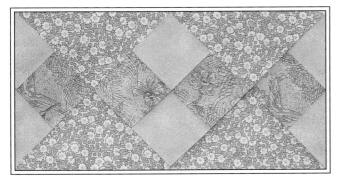

HOW TO CONSTRUCT THIS BORDER

This border is inspired by the Nine-Patch antique quilt on pages 6 and 7.

Sew light A to dark A (2 times). Reversing color placement, sew AA to AA. To opposite sides of AAAA, sew C. Sew light B to A (2 times); add B to the adjoining side (2 times). Sew C to ABB (2 times). Sew BABC to CAAAAC; add BABC to the opposite side.

DIAMOND LINK
full-size border

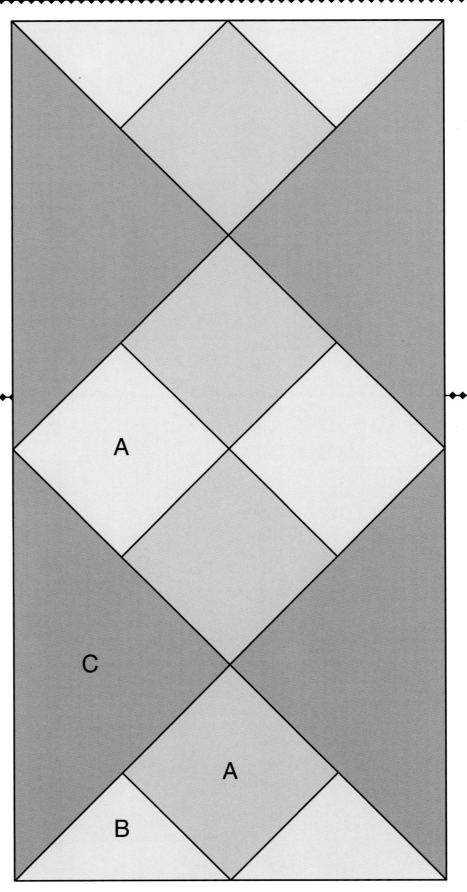

Stripes Around

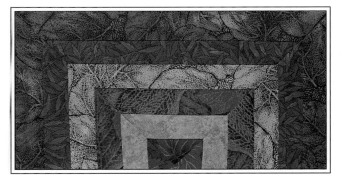

HOW TO CONSTRUCT THIS BORDER

Sew A to B. In alphabetical order, add C, D, E, and F. Sew Ar to Br. In alphabetical order, add Cr, Dr, Er, and Fr. Sew G to H. In alphabetical order, add I, J, K, and L. Sew ABCDEF to the left side of GHIJKL. Sew ArBrCrDrErFr to the right side of GHIJKL.

STRIPES AROUND
full-size border

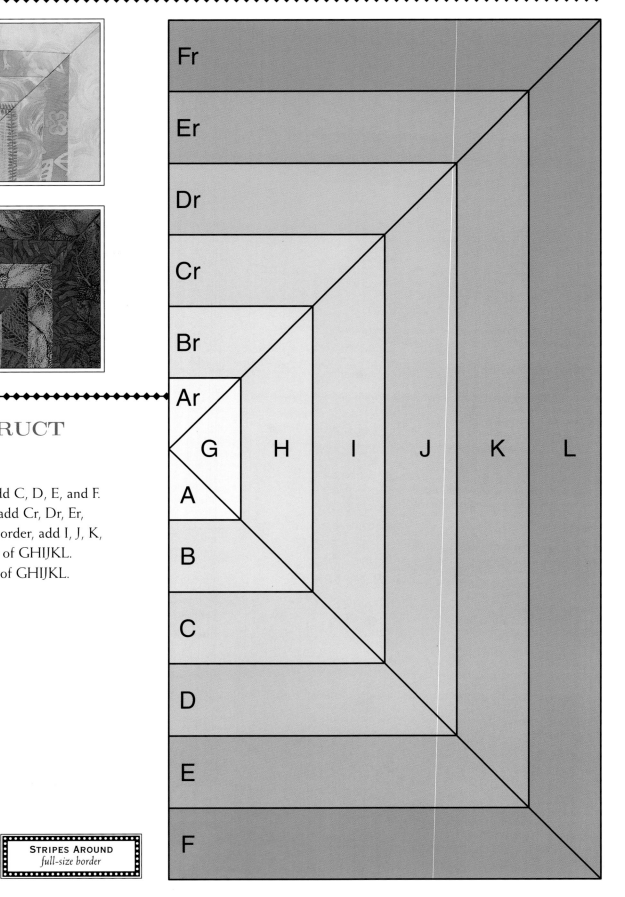

Daisy

HOW TO CONSTRUCT THIS BORDER

Sew light A to dark A (2 times). Sew dark B to the left side of one AA. Sew dark A to the right side of BAA. Sew dark B to the right side of other AA. Sew dark A to the left side of other AAB. Sew the short side of light B to the short side of dark B in Unit 1. Reversing the long side of B, sew the opposite short side of light B to the opposite short side of dark B in Unit 2. Sew Unit 1 BB to BAAA. Sew Unit 2 BB to AAAB. Sew BAAABB to the left side of C. Press the seam allowance toward BAAABB. Sew AAABBB to the right side of C. Press the seam allowance toward AAABBB. Fold C in half; press. Using the pressed line as a guide, lay out the appliqué pieces on C. Beginning with D and Dr, appliqué each piece in place alphabetically using matching threads.

DAISY
full-size border

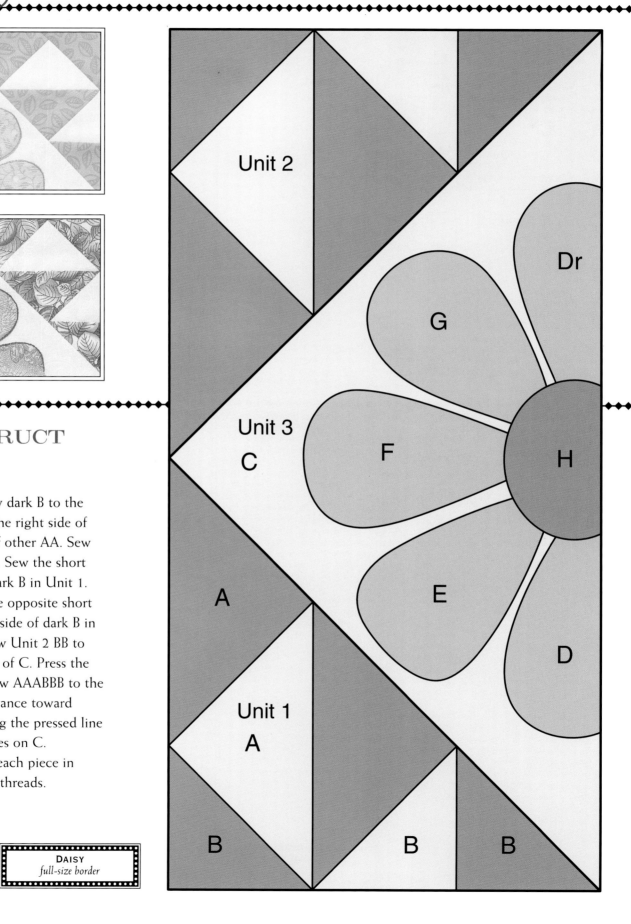

Spring Bloom

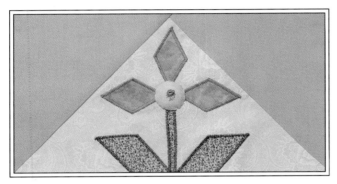

HOW TO CONSTRUCT THIS BORDER

Sew A to opposite short sides of B; press the seam allowance toward A. Fold B in half and press. Using the pressed line as a guide, lay out and appliqué the pattern pieces on B alphabetically, beginning with C.

SPRING BLOOM
full-size border

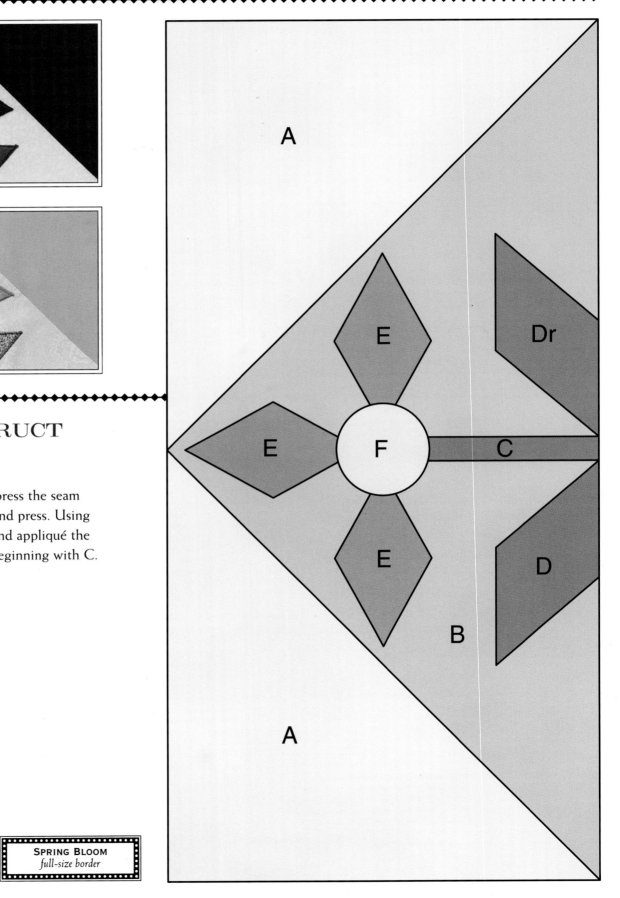

Flying Geese

HOW TO CONSTRUCT THIS BORDER

This border is inspired by the Nine-Patch antique quilt on pages 6 and 7.

Sew A to B (4 times); add A (4 times). Sew ABA to ABA (2 times). Sew ABAABA to ABAABA.

FLYING GEESE
full-size border

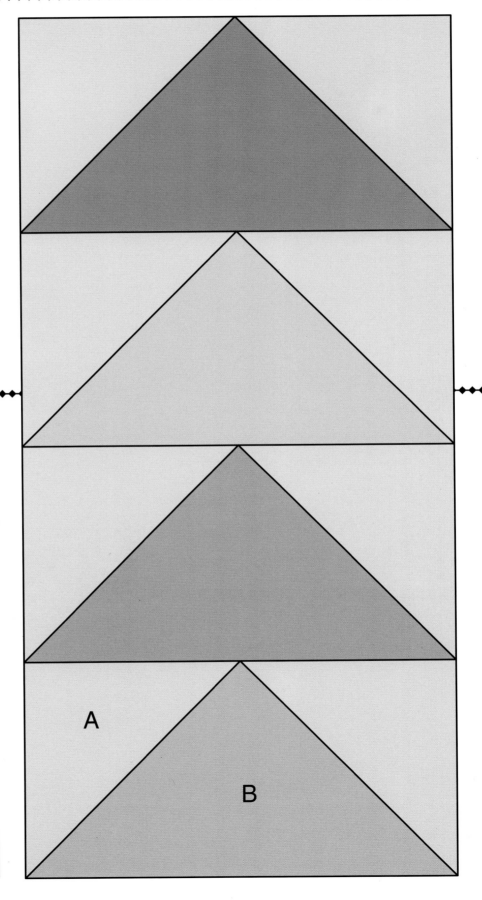

A

B

Fancy Flower

HOW TO CONSTRUCT THIS BORDER

This border is inspired by the Album antique quilt on page 12.

On a 9½-inch background square, carefully mark the placement of Pattern A. Appliqué Pattern A onto the background square, using matching thread. Beginning with Pattern B, appliqué each pattern alphabetically onto the background square, using matching threads. Repeat with enough blocks to fit the border length that is needed. Sew the blocks together to complete the border.

Prairie Points

HOW TO CONSTRUCT THIS BORDER

Pictured on page 200.

Press desired size fabric squares in half diagonally twice, right sides out. (Use four 3½-inch squares to place four Prairie Points along the edge of a 9-inch block.) Pin the raw edge of the triangles evenly along the edges of the quilt top. Lap adjacent edges or slip double-folds inside the single-folds. Stitch on seam line using a ¼-inch seam allowance.

PRAIRIE POINTS
border sample

A

B

C

D

E

E

F

F

F

Starry Scallop

D

A

B

C

This border is inspired by the antique quilt on page 201.

How to Construct This Border

To make one Starry Scallop border block in your chosen method of appliqué, appliqué A onto background D. Appliqué B to D. Appliqué C to B. The edges of the appliqué may be finished with machine stitching or hand embroidery.

STARRY SCALLOP
full-size border

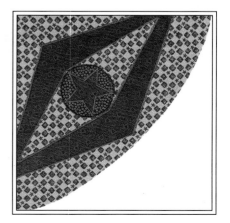

Letter Art

LEFT:

ALPHABET QUILT LETTER GRID
*from block on page 89.
Use grid to enlarge letters,
below left.*

BELOW LEFT:

ALPHABET QUILT LETTER PATTERNS
*Enlarge letters to fit grid
at left.*

BELOW RIGHT:

CRAZY QUILT EMBROIDERY LETTER PATTERNS
*Use alphabet for Crazy
Monogram block, page 128,
or personalize quilt blocks.*

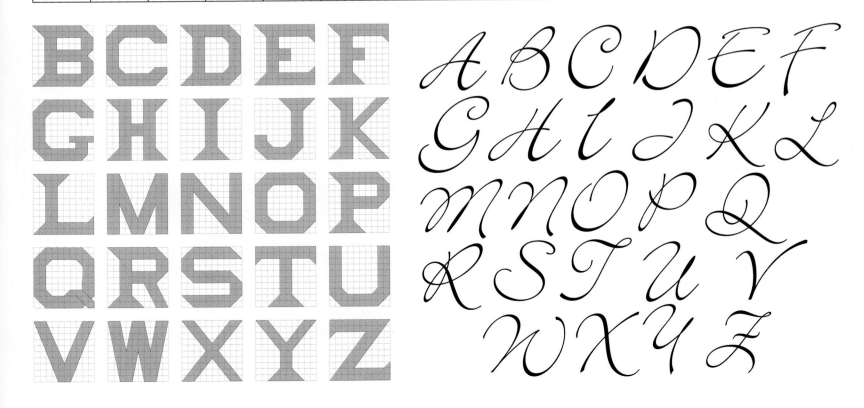

213

About the Quilt Collections

CRAZY ANN QUILT
see page 147

LIVING HISTORY FARMS
DES MOINES, IOWA

With over 300 historic quilts in its textile collection, Living History Farms treasures the past. Within the authentic surroundings visitors are privy to not only quilts but coverlets, blankets, household items, and clothing of men, women, and children within a 1700s Ioway Indian Farm, an 1850 Pioneer Farm, and a 1900 horse-powered Farm.

Because Living History Farms is an open-air museum and because textiles are sensitive elements, the staff use reproduction textiles in the historic sites.

Some of these reproductions are based on items in their collection. Part of the historic collection is on display during the annual quilt show, usually held in the fall.

Guests are encouraged to stroll the boardwalks of Living History Farms—a place where history can be experienced firsthand. For more information on event schedules and hours, please contact:

Living History Farms
2600 111th Street
Urbandale, IA 50322
515-278-5286
www.livinghistoryfarms.org

THE UNIVERSITY OF
NEBRASKA–LINCOLN

With a state-of-the-art storage facility and one of the few full-time curators in the United States dedicated to the care and exhibition of a quilt collection, the International Quilt Study Center (IQSC) at the University of Nebraska–Lincoln is highly praised and treasured by those who have an appreciation of quilts.

Its roots began in 1979 when Ardis and Robert James, formerly of Nebraska, happened upon a quilt festival in Michigan. Ardis found an antique Mariner's Compass quilt that piqued her interest, and she bought it. Within a few years, her passion for quilts grew, and she added to her collection until Robert joined her in her quest. Once they started seeking quilts together, the numbers grew quickly, and eventually they owned more than 1,000 contemporary and antique quilts.

The Jameses were instrumental in founding the International Quilt Study Center, donating nearly 950 quilts in 1997

along with a financial pledge to create the center that today encourages scholarship and nurtures the appreciation of quilts as art.

To expand the knowledge of quilt history and the use of quilts as a medium of artistic expression, the University of Nebraska–Lincoln offers graduate study in textile history and textile design with an emphasis in quilt studies. The International Quilt Study Center sponsors public exhibitions of art and antique quilts in partnership with museums and galleries worldwide. For more information on visiting the International Quilt Study Center or for a listing of the course schedule, please contact them at:

The University of Nebraska-Lincoln
International Quilt Study Center
234 Home Economics Building
Lincoln, NE 68583-0838
402-472-6549
http://quiltstudy.unl.edu

CRAZY PATCHWORK
see page 66

Sources, Resources, Credits

BATTING

Morning Glory Products/ Division of Carpenter Co.

Mountain Mist/Stearns Technical
100 Williams St.
Cincinnati, OH 45215
800-543-7173
E-mail: mountain.mist@ stearnstextiles.com
www.stearnstextiles.com

FABRIC DYE

Rit Dye, Best Foods Specialty Products
1437 West Morris St.
P.O. Box 21070
Indianapolis, IN 46221
317-231-8028

FABRICS

Bali Fabrics-Princess Mirah Design
800-783-4612
E-mail: BATIK@BALIFAB.COM
www.balifab.com

Benartex, Inc.
1359 Broadway
Suite 1100
New York, NY 10018
212-840-3250
www.benartex.com

Clothworks—A Division of Fabric Sales Co.
www.clothworks-fabrics.com

Cranston Printworks Co.
469 Seventh Avenue
New York, NY 10018
www.cranstonvillage.com

Dan River, Inc.
1065 Avenue of Americas
New York, NY 10018

Fabri-Quilt, Inc.
901 E. 14 Ave.
N. Kansas City, MO 64116
www.fabri-quilt.com

Hoffmann California Fabrics
25792 Obrero Dr.
Mission Viejo, CA 92691
See local quilt shops for fabrics.

Marcus Brothers Textiles, Inc.
980 Avenue of Americas
New York, NY 10018
212-354-8700
www.marcusbrothers.com

Moda/United Notions
13795 Hutton
Dallas, TX 75234
www.modafabrics.com

Northcott/Monarch
229 West 36th St.
New York, NY 10018
www.northcott.net

P & B Textiles
1580 Gilbreth Rd.
Burlingame, CA 94010
www.pbtex.com

Peter Pan Fabrics
11 East 36th St.
New York, NY 10016
800-854-5933

R.J.R. Fashion Fabrics
Purchased at local quilt shops
To view our complete fabric inventory visit:
www.rjrfabrics.com

NOTIONS

Prym-Dritz Corporation
P.O. Box 5028
Spartanburg, SC 29304

QUILTERS

Linda Beardsley, Margaret Sindelar, and Jan Temeyer

RESOURCES

American Patchwork & Quilting, Better Homes and Gardens Books, ©1985.

The Amish Quilt, Eve Wheatcroft Granick, Good Books, ©1994.

Aunt Jane of Kentucky, Eliza Calvert Hall, University Press of Kentucky, ©1995.

Better Homes and Gardens® American Patchwork & Quilting® magazine.

Better Homes and Gardens® America's Heritage Quilts, Meredith Press, ©1991.

Complete Guide to Quilting, Audrey Heard and Beverly Pryor, Creative Home Library in association with Meredith, ©1974.

Dating Fabric: A Color Guide 1800–1960, Barbara Smith, American Quilter's Society, ©1998.

Dictionary of Needlework, Sophia Caulfeild and Blanche Saward, Arno Press, Distributed by Crown Publishers, ©1972.

Friendship Quilting, Better Homes and Gardens® Books, ©1990.

Historic Quilts, New York: The American Historical Co., ©1939.

Labors of Love: America's Textiles and Needlework 1650-1930, Judith Reiter Weissman and Wendy Lavitt, Alfred A. Knopf Publishers, ©1987.

Nebraska Quilts & Quiltmakers, Ronald C. Naugle, University of Nebraska Press, ©1991.

Perfect Pineapples, Jane Hall and Dixie Haywood, C&T Publishing, ©1989.

Polly Prindle's Book of American Patchwork Quilts by Alice I. Gammell, Grosset & Dunlap, ©1973.

Quilter's Complete Guide, Marianne Fons and Liz Porter, Oxmoor House, ©2001.

Quilting for Beginners, Agnes Frank, Sterling Publishers, ©1990.

Reminiscences of Newcastle, Iowa 1848, Historical Dept. of IA, ©1921.

Treasury of Amish Quilts, Rachel and Kenneth Pellman, Good Books, ©1990.

Treasury of Mennonite Quilts, Rachel and Kenneth Pellman, Good Books, ©1992.

The Standard Book of Quilt Making and Collecting, Dover Publications, Inc., ©1949.

UNIVERSITY OF NEBRASKA QUILT REFERENCE NUMBERS:

Page 7	Album Quilt	1997.007.0153
Page 7	Nine-Patch Quilt	1997.007.0199
Page 8	Friendship Album Quilt	1997.007.0666
Page 8	Stars Quilt	1997.007.0313
Page 11	Ships of Maine Quilt	1997.007.0386
Page 11	Friendship Album Quilt	1997.007.0267
Page 12	Album Quilt	1997.007.0462
Page 12	Three-Pattern Applique Quilt	1997.007.0231
Page 61	Ohio Star Quilt	1997.007.0281
Page 61	Carolina Lily	1997.007.0042
Page 61	Floral Appliqué Quilt	1997.007.0349
Page 62	Texas Star with Tulip Var.	1997.007.0014
Page 62	Delectable Mountains	1997.007.0262
Page 65	Log Cabin	1997.007.0114
Page 65	Alphabet	1997.007.0324
Page 66	New York Beauty	1997.007.0124
Page 66	Crazy Patchwork	1997.007.0234
Page 103	Sawtooth Quilt	1997.007.0430
Page 103	Amish Quilt (Baskets)	1997.007.0436
Page 103	Amish Quilt (16-Patch)	2000.007.0018
Page 104	Tile Quilt	1997.007.0163
Page 104	Crazy Quilt	1997.007.0107
Page 107	Schoolhouse	1997.007.0314
Page 107	Log Cabin	1997.007.0127
Page 108	Memorial Album Quilt	1997.007.0252
Page 108	Single Irish Chain	1997.007.0363
Page 111	Road to Paris Variations	1997.007.0295
Page 145	Cornucopias	1997.007.0266
Page 145	Appliquéd Poppies	1997.007.0411
Page 145	Grandmother's Fan	1997.007.0036
Page 146	Baby Bunting Fans	1997.007.0366
Page 146	Postage Stamp, Trip Round The World	1997.007.0122
Page 149	Deco Shooting Star	1997.007.0218
Page 149	Martha's Vineyard	1997.007.0219
Page 150	Sunbonnet Sue	1997.007.0256
Page 150	Signature Quilt	1997.007.0148
Page 153	Fool's Puzzle	1997.007.0384

Better Homes and Gardens® Books An Imprint of Meredith® Books

Grandma's Best Full-Size Quilt Blocks

Editor: Carol Field Dahlstrom
Technical Editor: Susan M. Banker
Contributing Writers: Carol McGarvey, Lila Scott
Graphic Designer: Angela Haupert Hoogensen
Copy Chief: Terri Fredrickson
Managers, Book Production: Pam Kvitne, Marjorie J. Schenkelberg
Editorial Operations Manager: Karen Schirm
Contributing Copy Editor: Margaret Smith
Contributing Proofreaders: Diane Doro, Karen Brewer Grossman, Joellyn Witke
Photographer: Andy Lyons CameraWorks
Technical Illustrator: Chris Neubauer Graphics, Inc.
Electronic Production Coordinator: Paula Forest
Editorial and Design Assistants: Kaye Chabot, Mary Lee Gavin

Meredith® Books
Editor in Chief: James D. Blume
Design Director: Matt Strelecki
Managing Editor: Gregory H. Kayko

Director, Sales, Special Markets: Rita McMullen
Director, Sales, Premiums: Michael A. Peterson
Director, Sales, Retail: Tom Wierzbicki
Director, Book Marketing: Brad Elmitt
Director, Operations: George A. Susral
Director, Production: Douglas M. Johnston

Better Homes and Gardens® Magazine
Editor in Chief: Karol DeWulf Nickell

Meredith Publishing Group
President, Publishing Group: Stephen M. Lacy

Meredith Corporation
Chairman and Chief Executive Officer: William T. Kerr

Chairman of the Executive Committee: E. T. Meredith III

Copyright © 2002 by Meredith Corporation, Des Moines, Iowa. First Edition. All rights reserved. Printed in China. Library of Congress Control Number: 2001135113 ISBN: 0-696-21265-X

All of us at Better Homes and Gardens® Books are dedicated to providing you with information and ideas to create beautiful and useful projects. We welcome your comments and suggestions. Write to us at: Better Homes and Gardens Books, Crafts Editorial Department, 1716 Locust Street—LN112, Des Moines, IA 50309-3023.

If you would like to purchase any of our crafts, cooking, gardening, home improvement, or home decorating and design books, check wherever quality books are sold. Or visit us online: bhgbooks.com

Cover Photograph: Courtesy, University of Nebraska–Lincoln

215

Index